The

UNWRITTEN RULES

of the WORKPLACE

A GUIDE TO ETIQUETTE AND
ATTIRE FOR BUSINESSMEN

 The

UNWRITTEN RULES
of the WORKPLACE

CLINTON T. GREENLEAF III

EMERALD
BOOK CO.

Published by Emerald Book Company
Austin, TX
www.emeraldbookcompany.com

Distributed by Emerald Book Company

For ordering information or special discounts for bulk purchases, please contact Emerald Book Company at PO Box 91869, Austin, TX 78709, 512.891.6100.

Design and composition by Greenleaf Book Group LLC and Alex Head
Cover design by Greenleaf Book Group LLC

Publisher's Cataloging-In-Publication Data
(Prepared by The Donohue Group, Inc.)
Greenleaf, Clinton T.
    The unwritten rules of the workplace : a guide to etiquette and attire for businessmen / Clinton T. Greenleaf III. -- 1st ed.
    p. : ill. ; cm.
    Includes bibliographical references.
    ISBN: 978-1-934572-56-6
    1. Business etiquette. 2. Business communication. 3. Language in the workplace. 4. Grooming for men. 5. Male employees--Clothing. I. Title.
HF5389 .G74 2010
395/.52   2010930288

Part of the Tree Neutral™ program, which offsets the number of trees consumed in the production and printing of this book by taking proactive steps, such as planting trees in direct proportion to the number of trees used: www.treeneutral.com

TreeNeutral

Printed in the United States of America on acid-free paper
10 11 12 13 14 15   10 9 8 7 6 5 4 3 2 1

First Edition

CONTENTS

Part II: Applying for a Job

Part III: Office Etiquette

Part IV: Personal Interaction

Part V: Communication

PREFACE

In matters of style, swim with the current;
in matters of principle, stand like a rock.
— Thomas Jefferson

From the first grade through high school, I attended University School, right outside Cleveland, Ohio, and I have some great memories of my time there. From my first day, in 1980, we were instructed to learn and understand the school motto: Responsibility, Loyalty, and Consideration.

At the time I had no idea of the magnitude (or the full meaning) of these three seemingly simple words, but over the twelve years I spent there and the years that followed, I learned how important they were. My experiences proved, time and time again, that these three words were the keys to proper conduct. When I put my appreciation of these words to work in the business world, I was considered a "business etiquette expert" by the *Wall Street Journal*. Since then I've built a publishing company from the ground up, and it has become a successful, multi-million-dollar enterprise. Etiquette might not be the only reason you are hired, promoted, or are successful, but you will see in this book that it will help you get a job, develop your career, and fit well into any situation.

This book, and its previous editions, began as a collection of notes that I wrote to help a few of my friends in college get an edge on job interviews. The idea was to help young men who were smart and talented but needed some guidance with the basics of acting like a gentleman. Through no fault of their own, they had not been taught these unwritten rules and the tips that would help them abide by them successfully. At a time when many young men do not know the basics of professional appearance and conduct, those who are knowledgeable have a clear advantage. The great news is that anyone can learn how to act properly, and this book will teach you the fundamentals.

The essence of etiquette is knowing how to act properly in different situations. I look at it simply: Etiquette is a healthy mix of professionalism and personality. The best rules are the ones that build your credibility with your coworkers, clients, friends, and anyone else you come into contact with. Etiquette is knowing when to "turn it on" and when to "turn it off." My office is now a casual work environment; we wear business casual when a client comes, and I wear a suit when I do TV. While I prefer to be comfortable in shorts and a golf shirt, I do at times need to dress up. The rules of etiquette and professional appearance don't demand that I always wear a suit, just that I do it properly in the right situations.

Over the past thirteen years, I have received many letters from men thanking me for the extra boost of confidence they got from reading and referring to earlier editions of this book before important interviews and meetings. My goal in writing *The Unwritten Rules of the Workplace* was to provide the rules of etiquette and proper conduct needed to survive in the business world. I hope that everyone who reads this will be more confident once armed with the necessary information to dress and act professionally, like a true gentleman.

INTRODUCTION

Clothes make the man. Naked people have little or no influence in society.
—Mark Twain

Let's face it—in today's world, appearance and conduct matter. People are judged, at least initially, by the way they look. They earn their credibility based on how they act. Those who want to succeed take the time to look their best and act appropriately.

No matter your background, you can learn to look great and conduct yourself like a professional and a gentleman by reading this book. You will learn that attention to detail matters, not only in your career, but in all aspects of your life. The level of care reflected in your appearance and manners attracts positive attention and admiration, which fosters confidence. This attention to detail is a highly valued skill in the professional world and will also have a positive effect on your personal life.

Part I

APPEARANCE

WHY APPEARANCE MATTERS

Who decided that tying some fabric around your neck makes you look more serious, or that wearing shined shoes gives you the appearance of a go-getter? Research studies show that there is a strong correlation between a person's appearance and others' perceptions of his professional abilities. Proper appearance also includes creating symmetry and neatness within your wardrobe—it's proven that a symmetrical look is appealing to most people. A well-tied tie, a properly tucked-in shirt, and well-shined shoes are a huge boost to your look—the first impression that will remain in most people's minds long after they meet you.

Former FBI agent and expert behavioral analyst Joe Navarro tells the story of a study that showed just how important your appearance is to how you are perceived. Researchers found that a jaywalker dressed in a clean, neat business suit was significantly more likely to be followed into the street by other pedestrians than a jaywalker dressed in jeans, rumpled trousers, or otherwise unprofessional, "low status" clothing (see "Jaywalking as a Function of Model Behavior," *Personality and Social Psychology Bulletin*, Vol. 16, No. 2, 320–330, 1990). There is no question that wearing a suit adds to your credibility.

The derivation and theories of societal grooming standards are not the point of this book, so it will not delve deeply into why the standards matter. As a reader, simply accept that they do. This book takes the stance that although individualism and self-expression are important, for most of us, dressing appropriately in the professional environment is necessary for success. While being well dressed is not enough to ensure success, an unprofessional appearance will almost guarantee failure. This book does not aim to tell you what you must do or wear, but to guide you in what is considered acceptable and preferred today, and help you learn what it takes to display a professional image.

Yes, there are a growing number of companies (including the one I founded, Greenleaf Book Group) that have casual work environments, but there are still times you will need to dress up. Even if you don't wear a suit to work every day, chances are you'll need to from time to time. Knowing how to do so properly is a great skill.

When it comes to etiquette, you also need to know when to "turn it on" and when to "turn it off." This is the case with not just your clothing, but also your sense of humor and attitude. There are times to be funny or dress with flair, and times to be conservative, especially with your wardrobe. Knowing what to wear — and when — is essential.

In the professional world, a suit is normal dress. The casual workplace has changed this tradition somewhat, but the general rule is still in place: When you are in a professional setting, wearing a tailored suit is a good start. No matter how polished your etiquette may be, if you look underdressed, others will not take you seriously.

Your wardrobe, then, should consist of well-tailored jackets and pants, matching ties, dress shirts, and a few pairs of well-shined shoes. Even though you may have a number of "fun" suits and ties with bold patterns, images, or colors, you should try to maintain a conservative look with standard-color suits of navy and charcoal and a professional-looking tie. The office is usually not the place to show your modern sense of style or collection of funny ties.

SHOES

Let's start with shoes. A great shine on your shoes can really enhance your professional image. The trick to a sparkling shoeshine is not elbow grease but technique. Once you have learned the technique, your shoes will stay shined, and your overall appearance will be notably improved.

First, buy some shoe polish that matches the color of your shoes. You can find polishes that match all colors of shoes, including black, brown, cordovan, oxblood, etc.

Place a few old newspapers on the floor before you start. You'll also need a cotton rag (an old T-shirt will do), a bit of water, and about thirty minutes per shoe (for the first time; ten minutes each time after that). Mentally separate each shoe into seven sections: (1) toe, (2) right front, (3) right back, (4) heel, (5) left back, (6) left front, and (7) tongue (figure 1). You will be working on only one of these sections at a time.

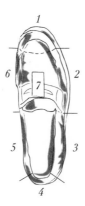

fig. 1 — The parts of a shoe

Open the polish tin and fill the top cover with lukewarm water. Take your rag and wrap it tightly around your right index and middle fingers (figure 2).

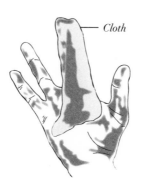

Cloth

fig. 2 — Wrap the cloth around index and middle fingers.

Touch your fingers to the water in the lid, and then smack them against your left palm to make sure the cloth is damp, but not too wet. Make a few circles in the polish with the moist rag. Now, using light pressure, apply the polish in a circular motion to the first section of the shoe (figure 3).

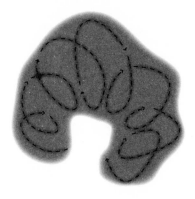

fig. 3 — Polish with a circular motion.

The trick here is to make small, tight circles as your fingers move around the section you're working on. As you apply the polish to your shoe, it will blur any existing shine. This indicates that the polish is filling every pore in the leather. By moving in circles, you will compact the polish in each pore. Once all pores are filled with polish, a shine will become visible as light is reflected from the smooth, flat surface (figure 4).

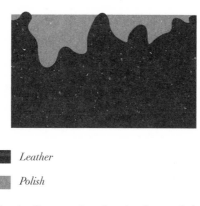

■ *Leather*

■ *Polish*

*fig. 4 — Cross section showing how polish
smoothes out rough leather*

Once you have applied polish to the first section, move your fingers to a clean part of the rag. Wet it as described earlier. Using water only, make the same polishing motions with a little less pressure on the same side of the shoe. You should notice the beginning of a nice shine. This buffing action will further compact the polish and smooth it into the pores of the leather.

When you polish each shoe for the first time, repeat the process (starting with new polish and then buffing it) two more times per section. Once a week, re-shine each section. This will take only about ten minutes and will keep your shoes looking great.

Another way to make your shoes look their best is to use edge dressing. This is basically a paint or dye that coats the side of the sole. It seals and protects, and gives your shoes a finished look. There are many types available, but Kiwi Honor Guard Edge Dressing is the best. Be careful with edge dressing, though, since it is a permanent dye and stains very easily. Remember to put newspaper on the floor, and apply the dressing only to the outer walls of the soles, not on the bottom. To fill the area where the leather meets the sole, use a cotton swab to apply the edge dressing (figure 5). Be sure not to touch the leather. Once a week, touch up any areas that may have become scuffed, which happens most often at the toe and heel.

— *Edge Dressing*

fig. 5 — Carefully apply edge dressing to the shoe.

12

After three or four months of constant wear and regular polishing, your shoes will become more difficult to shine. The polish will begin to build up in some areas and eventually crack and fall off. This leaves uneven layers of polish and a dull shine. To remedy this, you will need to break down the finish. This is a relatively simple but messy process, so, again, lay down some newspaper. You will also need a few rags, a toothbrush, and a can of shaving cream.

First, remove any laces from your shoes so they will not interfere with the process. Rub the shaving cream gently into the leather, covering it completely. If you have a gel-type shaving cream, spray it on your hand and make sure to work up a good lather before applying it. After both shoes are covered with the cream, set them aside for about four hours to break down the chemical bonds of the polish and allow it to detach from the leather. At the same time, the cream will condition the shoe as it moisturizes and softens the leather.

After four hours have passed, take the rags and carefully wipe the cream off the shoes. You will notice that your rags will collect some old polish along with the cream. Be sure to wipe the shaving cream off completely; if it stays on the shoe, it will flake off after you have re-polished and will ruin the shine.

Use the toothbrush to clean the shaving cream out of the small creases in the leather and the area where the sole meets the leather.

You should notice after breaking down the finish that the leather is suppler and has a duller shine. This process is beneficial to the shoe and can extend its life by as much as 50 percent.

The next step is to buy some shoe cream. It comes in a smaller jar than polish but will be available in the same colors. First, cover the leather with the shoe cream. Use a rag and polish in the circular motion described earlier. When you have covered the shoe with cream, brush it in with a horsehair brush. If you don't have a brush, you can use a clean part of the rag. Let the shoe sit for about an hour so the cream can get to work. Then, simply repeat the process of shining as described in the beginning of this chapter.

You will also discover that your shoes will last two to three times longer than usual if you buy at least two pairs and alternate them daily (figure 6). When your shoes are not worn, cedar shoe trees will help them keep their form and allow them to dry and air out completely. Shoe trees are essentially molds of feet that you place in your shoes when you are not wearing them. Without a shoe tree, the leather will sink down and begin to shrink as the shoes lie unworn, since the sweat from your feet soaks the leather and can cause it to become misshapen.

Tuesday

Wednesday

Thursday

Monday

Friday

fig. 6—Alternate shoes throughout the workweek.

A good shoe tree will push the leather and help it retain its intended shape. It will also help dry the leather and keep your sweat from damaging and cracking the shoe. One other benefit of shoe trees is that they help keep your shoes smelling good; quality shoe trees are made of cedar that absorbs both sweat and odor. You can buy a cheap plastic pair of shoe trees for less than ten dollars, but they will be essentially useless. This type is flimsy, hollow, and will not adjust well to your shoes. Good shoe trees, like the Woodlore model, run twenty-five to thirty dollars a pair. This one has a split toe that expands to fit the width of the shoe and an overhang heel for easy removal.

If you work in a professional office environment, be sure to buy leather-soled shoes. Leather-soled shoes have a certain quality about them that rubber-soled shoes do not. The marginal improvement in your comfort you get with rubber soles will not replace the loss of credibility you will incur by wearing them.

If you live in a snowy climate, the salt used to melt snow on the ground will invariably get on your shoes. Often, this salt accumulates on leather shoes and wreaks havoc on a good shine. The white stain is almost impossible to get off, but, worse, the salt will destroy your shoes.

The best way to remove this salt is a fifty-fifty mixture of water and white vinegar. Mix the two in the top of a shoe polish tin. Dab a clean rag in the mixture and rub it into the salt lines of the shoe. After it looks like you have removed it, allow it to dry for about twenty minutes. Check to be sure all of it is removed. If any of the salt stains remain, simply repeat the process. Once all the salt is removed, apply some shoe cream to the treated area and polish it as usual.

A good shine and a few well-cared-for pairs of leather-soled shoes will clearly illustrate your attention to detail and professionalism. This is an extremely easy way to increase your credibility and show others that you care about your appearance.

SHIRTS

Although casual Fridays allow us to relax our clothes once a week, chances are you need to wear a dress shirt to work most of the time. A pressed dress shirt shows that you care about your appearance and helps you look more fit. Have your shirts profession-ally washed and ironed. It may seem like an unnec-essary expense, but the benefits are more than worth it. For less than two dollars a day, your shirts will be laundered and ironed properly. If you check around, you may also find dry cleaners who will pick up and deliver directly to your home or office.

For those times when you have to iron your shirt but cannot find a twenty-four-hour cleaner, how-ever, here are the basic steps. The only tools you'll need are an iron and an ironing board. If, for some reason, you do not have an iron, your best (and only) bet is to turn on the shower as hot as possible, hang your shirt in the bathroom, and close the door. This will steam your shirt and take out some of the wrinkles. If you are staying at a hotel, check for an iron and ironing board; there should be one in your closet or at the front desk. If you have an iron and not the board, get a thick towel and place it on any hard surface.

Check the tag on your shirt to make sure that the fabric can handle steam ironing. Now, pour some distilled water into the iron. If the iron does not have a hole on top for adding water, use a spray bottle instead. Using steam as you iron will keep the fabric lightly damp.

The part to start with is the collar, and it is quite important. Flatten the collar and move from the points to the back of the neck on both sides. Take extra care to be sure that the points are straight.

To iron the shoulder, place it on the corner of the board or table to simulate your shoulder. Then, place the sleeves on the ironing board or table and iron each sleeve on both sides. Mist the fabric and place the iron at the shoulder. Pull the iron from the shoulder seam to the cuff.

From the shoulder, move to the front of the shirt, starting on the side with buttons. Stretch the shirt across the board, spray lightly with water, and move the iron from the shoulder down to the bottom. Be careful when you iron between the buttons; it is easy to melt or snap them. Now iron the back of the shirt; again, iron from the shoulder to the bottom. You can now finish with the other front half of the shirt. Keep in mind that the placard—the piece of fabric with the buttonholes in it—should be kept very flat and stretched. Because it double the thickness of the rest of the shirt, it's often hard to get it to lay flat; however, it is very noticeable when the placard is not correctly ironed, so practice at it and get it flat.

A properly pressed shirt must be tucked in well. After you button it, gently pull down and out on the front of the shirt (figure 7). This will straighten the button line so it is directly in the middle of your body. Now, slide your hands around your sides from your front to your back to bunch any loose cloth in the back (figure 8). Take the excess cloth in your hands and fold it over toward the outside. Holding the shirt in position, pull up your pants and lock the shirt in place (figure 9). This trick will keep your front free of wrinkles and folds, and the fold in the back will nicely hide any extra fabric.

fig. 7—The shirt front

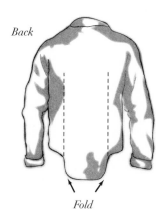

fig. 8—Move loose fabric from the front of the shirt to the back.

Excess Fabric   *Excess Fabric*

fig. 9—Bunch and fold over loose fabric at back of shirt before tucking.

When you buy your shirts, be sure that the material is opaque. It is not appropriate to see chest hair or a design on a T-shirt through the fabric. Also, wear only long-sleeved dress shirts with a suit. If you feel the need to have shorter sleeves, you can always roll them up.

A T-shirt should be worn underneath most dress shirts. The T-shirt should have a full neck and short sleeves. V-necks and tank tops are visible under most dress shirts and look inappropriate. Wearing a T-shirt may make you a little warmer, but deal with the heat and cover yourself; it does matter.

It's almost impossible to look professional with a transparent shirt worn with nothing underneath.

Many shirts have collars and cuffs that contrast in color with the rest of the shirt—for example, a blue shirt with white collar and cuffs. These shirts come in and out of style and are acceptable only in certain circles. A good rule is to watch what other people in your office wear and notice how certain styles are received. If your office is stylish, feel free to wear such a shirt. If your office is very conservative, you may wish to keep your shirts a solid color. By keeping an eye on the general attire of the office, you demonstrate that you are paying attention to detail and enhancing your professional appearance. Until you get a feel for the culture of your workplace, it makes sense to play by the rules and save your self-expression for your own time.

There are several types of shirt collars to choose from. The four basic types are the button-down collar, the point collar, the spread collar, and the sculptured collar. Each type is considered appropriate for business. The right choice depends on personal taste. One word of caution, though: If you wear button-down collars, make sure that both sides are buttoned. If your collars are not buttoned down, get your cleaner to heavily starch them. The starch will keep your collar from curling up and looking unprofessional. Remember that your image is always under scrutiny, and a neglected collar can make you look sloppy.

Many shirts come with collar stays—the long, thin pieces of metal or thick plastic, usually arrow-shaped, that slide into a slot in the underside of the collar—which add some stiffness to the collar. Be sure to take them out when the shirt is cleaned. If you forget, or if they get bent, replace them. You can buy collar stays online or from fine clothing stores, and you can also buy magnetic collar stays, which use a small magnet to keep your collar straight and in place on your shirt.

There are a number of companies that offer custom-made shirts. The general rule is that if they fit you well, off-the-rack shirts are fine. If your frame is unique and you find it difficult to find shirts that fit, custom shirts may be for you. Some people consider custom-made shirts superior, but the majority of men wear off-the-rack clothes and still look professional.

TIES

Most professional men must wear a tie. Unfortunately, 80 percent do it poorly. This is often the result of a half-Windsor knot (also known as the four-in-hand), which makes ties appear asymmetrical (figure 10). Most executives would agree that a half-Windsor knot looks unprofessional and that a full Windsor looks best for business (figure 11).

fig. 10 — The half-Windsor knot

fig. 11 — The full Windsor knot

To tie a full Windsor knot, put your tie around your neck with the wide base on the right and the thin end on the left. (The figures show what you will see if you stand in front of a mirror.) Pull the tie so that the bottom of the thin section is even with the third button down from the top of your shirt. Now cross the wide section over the thin section, making an X (figure 12). Pull the wide section across the X then up through the loop between the tie and your collar, and then drop it down on the right side (figure 13). Bring the long end of the tie behind the knot to the left side (figure 14). Pull the long end through the loop between your tie and collar, and drop it down on the right side. At this point you should have a V-shaped knot. Bring the long end across the front of the knot (figure 15). Bring it back up through the loop behind the knot (figure 16), then tuck it through the middle front part of the knot. You've now correctly tied your tie (figure 17)!

fig. 12—Pull the wide section over the thin.

Back

fig. 13—Pull the wide section across the X then up through the loop between the tie and your collar.

Back

fig. 14—Bring the long end of the tie behind the knot to the left side.

fig. 15—Pull the long end in front of the V-shaped knot.

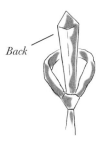

Back

fig. 16—Pull wide section up through the loop behind the knot.

fig. 17—A correctly tied tie

The first few times you use this method, you might have a little bit of trouble getting it to sit properly. The wide part should be longer than the thin part, and the tip of the wide part should be even with the bottom of your belt buckle. Be sure that the bottom of the tie does not end above your buckle or extend too far below the belt. Do not worry if you do not get it right on the first few tries; over time it will become second nature.

Although prevalent through the 1960s, tie clips and tiepins are no longer in style. If your tie is properly tied, it will remain in place without a clip or pin. However, if you want to wear a clip or pin with your suit, feel free; simply understand that it conveys an older image. Ties are usually best when understated, with muted colors or designs. The bold, flashy ties that used to be common have come out of style.

Most men only wear bow ties with tuxedos, but tying a bow tie is considered an art. To learn it, follow the instructions below.

The tie we will use is half white, half black, as seen in figure 18. Begin by wrapping the white end around the middle of the black side, and pull the ends out to the side, much like the first step of tying a shoe (figure 19). Now take the white end and fold it three ways, as seen in figure 20. This will form the front of the bow, a sort of T. Press the white bow against your throat, and wrap the black piece over the front and middle of the tie (figure 21). Make the same kind of three-fold T with the end of the black piece. Now, pull the black bow behind the white bow, between the fabric closest to your neck and the white bow (figure 22). You should end up with two bows, the white in front and the black in back (figure 23). Now pull gently on the bows to tighten the knot, and you have a formal bow tie!

fig. 18 — The untied bow tie

fig. 19 — Wrap white end around the middle of the black side.

fig. 20 — Fold white end three ways.

fig. 21 — Wrap the black side over the front of the tie.

fig. 22 — Fold black side behind the white bow.

fig. 23 — A correctly tied bow tie

Although you may not have many opportunities to wear one, the ability to tie a real bow tie will add credibility to your character. Few men know how. Some professionals wear bow ties often and make them their style, but, professionally speaking, bow ties are definitely not mainstream, and can be the mark of an eccentric.

PANTS

Wearing pants seems easy enough, right? While pants are not nearly as problematic as ties or shirts, they do require a bit of care. In the professional world, you will spend most of your time sitting, which causes your pants to wear faster than your jacket. This creates a mismatch in color and quality between your jacket and pants, which looks quite unprofessional. Although this wear is somewhat inevitable, there are steps you can take to slow the process.

Carry your wallet in the breast pocket of your jacket instead of your pants to prevent your pant pocket from wearing out. Another option is to carry a money clip for your bills and a cardholder for your credit cards and driver's license. If you put one in each front pant pocket, you will be able to carry your valuables without seriously damaging your pockets. You might also look at the new money clips that hold both credit cards and cash and are slim enough to keep your pants safe.

Keys and coins are another pocket killer. If you must carry keys, limit them to the ones you must have to make it through the workday. Both keys and coins will leave outlines on your pants or make holes in your pockets if they are carried in the same pocket day after day. It is considered unprofessional to walk with coins and keys clinking around in your pocket, so limit the amount of coins you have and keep them in a pocket separate from your keys.

When you remove your suit after the workday, folding your pants properly will ensure a good crease and fewer wrinkles. Begin by holding your pants upside down and lining up all four seams (figure 24). Pull the front and back of the pant out at the cuff, keeping the seams together. The fold should fall on the natural crease of the pants. Slip the pants onto a hanger, replace the jacket, and hang them up in your closet.

fig. 24—Hold pants upside down and line up seams before hanging.

Pressing your pants becomes an important part of keeping a professional appearance once wrinkles become noticeable. Pressed pants will make your suit look sharper and illustrate your attention to detail. The good news is that pressing your pants does not necessarily mean dry-cleaning them. You can press them with an iron in about a minute and bring them back to life. Before you do, however, make sure to check the care label in your suit to be sure the material can be ironed.

Line up the seams of your pants as detailed above, lay them on an ironing table, and press out the wrinkles. Depending on the fabric, consider using a pressing cloth or turning the pants inside out to avoid burning them or leaving a shiny surface. Either will look extremely unprofessional.

THE "GIG-LINE"

As you get ready to buckle your belt, look at your shirt. Your "gig-line" should be straight. The gig-line is a vertical line that runs the length of your body from your zipper to your collar. This line has three major components: pants, belt, and shirt. The right side of your zipper should be even with the button on the top of your pants. Use this as your guide. Next, take the button line of your shirt and pull it down so that the right edge of the line is even with your zipper line. The third part requires that you adjust the belt so that the right edge of your buckle is even with your pant and shirt line. Your tie will follow the gig-line naturally and end up at the bottom of your belt buckle. This is a straight gig-line, and this symmetry really makes a difference in overall professional appearance (figure 25).

Gig-Line

fig. 25 — A straight "gig-line"

SUITS

When you set out to buy a suit, you need to be prepared. You have to go into the store armed with good information and an understanding of what you want. First, know which of the three basic suit cuts will fit you best. The American cut is has a vented, three-button jacket with no padding in the shoulders. The British cut has a two-button jacket that is slightly tapered and has more shape in the shoulders. The European cut—or Italian cut—is a sleek cut that features a strongly tapered waist, padded shoulders, and no vents.

If money is a bit tight, look at the private-label suits from high-end stores. These are made with great care and are reasonably priced. Quality means it'll last longer, giving you a lower cost per wearing. The sales people and on-staff tailors there will help you find the suit you're looking for. It's always better to get one high-quality suit than two cheap ones—the one will last longer than the two every time.

When you buy suits, you must first choose the right jacket size; the average American male is about a 42. The "drop" is the difference between jacket size and pant waist. Most suits have a drop of seven inches, so a size-42 suit will usually come with a 35-inch waist.

The vent is the slit in the back of the suit, which is usually about six inches long. The purpose of the vent is to allow a man with a larger bottom to fit into a suit in which the shoulders are not very wide. For example, a pear-shaped man would want to wear a suit with vents, but a chiseled Marine has little need for vents. As a general rule, full suits have two vents, regulars have one, and athletic suits have none. If you have a large backside, you should consider a suit with at least one vent.

The question of a single- or double-breasted suit is common, and it is really a matter of personal preference. If you like a broad-chested look, then a double-breasted suit is right for you. Although double-breasted suits are considered more formal, they are less common in the professional workplace. If you do wear a double-breasted suit, remember to keep it buttoned at all times.

There are two basic variables when it comes to suit pants: pleats and cuffs. A pleat is the fold in the pants just below the beltline between the zipper and the pocket. The standard for professional suit pants is a double pleat. Make sure that the pleats lay flat and are not pulled apart. If they are pulled apart, this is a sign that you need wider pants.

Most suit pants are sold with cuffs, and they are considered standard on dress pants. Unless you have a good reason not to like cuffs, you can get them on your next pair of suit pants.

Finally, when purchasing a suit, be sure to bring an honest friend along with you to give you useful feedback on the fit of the suits. Try on several different styles and sizes, and do not skimp on quality. And remember: As soon as you purchase your suit, take it to a reputable tailor and have it tailored to fit you perfectly.

JACKETS

The key to a professional-looking suit is finding a high-quality, well-tailored jacket that fits your frame and is a basic color. Although some businessmen remove their suit jackets during the day, the jacket is an integral part of the professional wardrobe. Make sure to hang up your jacket when you are not wearing it, including the drive to work. While sitting at your desk, remove your jacket if protocol allows, and make sure you keep a few high-quality hangers in your office. When you wear your jacket, button only the top button. Walking with an open jacket looks sloppy, and buttoning two buttons looks too rigid. (If it's a three-button suit, button only the middle button when walking.) When you sit down while wearing a jacket, be sure to unbutton it. If you are interested in a classy look, consider a pocket handkerchief that matches your tie.

A jacket that fits properly is the most basic item in your professional wardrobe. It is, however, not cheap. But, as with all clothing, paying for quality is the best way to go. First, find the style of suit that best fits your frame. There are three main styles: athletic, regular, and full. If you have a typical American male frame, you will probably wear a regular-style suit. If you are in great shape, the athletic style may be the best. If you have a more portly figure, try the full cut.

To find the right sleeve length, stretch your arms out in front of you. The edge of the sleeve should touch the wrist bone that sticks up on the outside of your arm. The shirt underneath should extend a half-inch beyond the edge of the jacket when your arms are outstretched (figure 26).

fig. 26 — The shirt should extend about a half-inch beyond the jacket sleeve.

To get the right jacket length, stand with your hands straight down and your fingers curled as if to hold a pen. The jacket bottom should just touch your fingers where the pen would sit.

Try to buy the highest-quality suit you can afford; it should look good on you and be a basic color, like navy blue or charcoal gray. Black, olive green, and light gray are also acceptable in some professions.

Once you have purchased the right suit, go to a qualified tailor and have it altered to fit your body. When your suit comes back from the tailor, search for small pieces of loose thread improperly cut in the factory or by the tailor. These little strings are sometimes referred to euphemistically as "pendants." Good hiding places for these threads are near buttons, buttonholes, and on and near seams (figure 28).

fig. 27 — Clip loose threads around buttons and buttonholes.

Use nail clippers to cut the threads as close to the body of the fabric as possible. Finding them before someone else does is a good idea.

FORMAL WEAR

Black-tie events are still common in business and must be taken seriously. As a man, you'll have it pretty easy at these parties. A tux, cummerbund, bow tie, white pleated shirt, and patent leather shoes are the norm. The only real choice you have with your tux is the color of the bow tie and cummerbund (the large belt-like object that wraps around your waist). Black is considered standard and safe, but you may choose to purchase a few extra colors or patterns for your wardrobe.

Be sure to wear the cummerbund with the folds facing up. If you have a large stomach, do not try to wear a cummerbund; wear a vest. You'll also need to buy pleated tuxedo shirts; your usual white dress shirt will not work. Studs, the little knobs that go in the buttonholes on your shirt, are usually appropriate to wear with a tuxedo.

A white-tie event is more formal and requires a longer jacket (also called a tailcoat, or "tails"), a white bow tie, and a white vest. The rest of the wardrobe is the same as for a black-tie occasion, except that the cummerbund is not worn. You may see the phrase "black tie optional" on some invitations. This used to mean that you had the option of wearing tails or a standard tuxedo. Now, it is usually interpreted to mean that you may wear a tuxedo or a suit. To be on the safe side and look your best, wear a tuxedo; you'll be in great company.

Many professionals do not need formal wear, but the formal party is still a staple of many businesses. For most young men, it makes sense to rent tuxedos through their high school years. But as a general rule, as soon as you stop growing, you should consider buying your own tuxedo. If you are often invited to very formal events, consider also purchasing a tails jacket. If you do buy a tuxedo, be sure to have it tailored so that it fits you well, as you would a regular suit. You will look terrible wearing formal wear if it is poorly tailored.

Whether you are buying or renting, make sure the jacket and pants are black. You can be as colorful as you want with your tie and cummerbund, but colored tuxedos are not appropriate. This black rule applies to your feet as well: Your socks and your shoes should both be black. If your usual black dress shoes are well shined, you might be able to wear them with your tux. However, you could also consider buying a patent leather pair to go with your tuxedo.

Many professionals choose not to attend formal functions because they do not know how to dress properly. Do not limit your career simply because of a lack of information. Because so many people are uncomfortable in this setting, wearing formal wear properly can really give you a leg up.

CLEANING YOUR CLOTHES

Stains and spots on your clothes are a fact of life. What follows is a general guide on what you can use to remove certain spots.

Some paper cuts or shaving nicks can go unde-tected until blood appears on your shirt. As soon as you notice a bloodstain, blot it with a paper towel, and then run the fabric under cold water for a few minutes. As early as possible, wash the fabric with color-safe bleach. It's also a good idea to keep a few Tide sticks in your desk and briefcase.

Deodorant stains should be blotted with white

vinegar, and then the fabric washed with color-safe bleach in the hottest water allowable (check the label for the recommended temperature). Old perspiration stains that have caused the fabric to yellow should also be blotted with white vinegar. Fresh perspiration stains may be blotted with ammonia water (one teaspoon of ammonia per quart of water). After blotting, soak the fabric in cold water, and then wash it in the hottest water allowable for the fabric.

During the workday, other stains can occur. In general, most stains can be cleaned by blotting—not rubbing—the stained area, soaking the fabric in cold water, and then washing it with color-safe bleach. Coffee stains can be treated in this manner, as can stains from chocolate, fruit juices, and soft drinks. Ink stains from ballpoint pens can be removed with hairspray. Simply spray the spot, let it soak into the fabric, and then wash the garment with color-safe bleach.

In caring for your clothes, again, you must be willing to pay the price necessary to keep your appearance impeccable. If you tend to be thrifty, you might be tempted to wear your shirts two or three times before getting them cleaned. Don't do it. Pay the extra money to wear a clean shirt every day. True, they will wear out faster, but wrinkles and spots will destroy not only your appearance but your credibility as a professional as well.

On the other hand, there is no set rule for how often you must clean your suits. Some suggest cleaning after one to three wearings; others say you can wait up to ten wearings. A common recommendation is to have a suit dry-cleaned at least once per season. As a general rule, you can wear your suits until you feel they are dirty and need to be cleaned. This usually means about five wearings, but make sure you feel comfortable with the cleanliness of your wardrobe. When you do dry-clean your suits, have the pants and jacket done together to ensure that the color continues to match.

ACCESSORIES

Now that your clothes are set, you need accessories. For starters, you need a business watch. This is a watch that looks professional with your suits, but is not too flashy. Leather and metal bands (gold, silver, and stainless steel) are good options, but avoid digital faces and plastic bands. Another important accessory is a leather belt. You will need one black belt and one brown belt (or a single convertible belt) with a nice silver or gold buckle. Remember that unless you are a cowboy or oil tycoon, you should keep the buckle size small for your professional environment.

Many professionals look great wearing suspenders (also called braces). Suspenders are a substitute for a belt, so wear one or the other, but not both. To wear suspenders properly, you'll need to pay to have buttons sewn into your pants to anchor the straps. No self-respecting professional (or even clown) wears clip-on suspenders. The color of your suspenders should match or complement your tie. As usual, choosing a solid color or basic pattern makes matching much easier. Also remember that outlandish colors may not be appropriate.

Buy a high-quality pen and avoid carrying a cheap pen during any interview or meeting. You can find a nice pen for about ten dollars, but don't be afraid to pay more for quality. A prestigious pen will really make you look good, just as a cheap pen can take away from your professional appearance. Montblanc, Waterman, and Cross are among the premiere manufacturers of high-quality pens.

Along with the pen, it is advisable to carry a leather-bound portfolio for important documents and your business card. This will help you carry loose papers in a professional-looking way at all times. If you find a need to carry several items, a leather or metal briefcase can be a fine accessory. Make sure, however, that it looks professional and not like an old gym bag.

Cologne should be used sparingly since people are turned off by an overpowering scent. As a general rule, use about half the amount you would use if you were going on a date. Put it on about fifteen minutes before you leave your house, as it takes a few minutes to dissipate. Use it to enhance your appearance, not dominate it.

Clean hands are imperative in business. While a manicure is not necessary (although some business-men do get manicures), it is important to keep your hands and fingernails clean. Your fingernails should be trimmed (not bitten) cleanly just above the quick, the place where your fingernail meets your skin. Give yourself about one-sixteenth of an inch of white at the end of each nail.

To always look your best, consider keeping an extra dress shirt, tie, and umbrella in your office or car. Stains on your shirts and ties are inevitable. Having extras handy will add a level of security to your professional appearance. The umbrella will keep your suit dry; a hard rain can really ruin a suit. Also, keep a few toothpicks in your car and briefcase. Few things are as embarrassing as belatedly noticing that you have part of your last meal in your teeth. Consider keeping some fresh gum or mouthwash around to help control your breath.

Be very careful about wearing too much jewelry. Wedding rings, college rings, and military rings are acceptable. Bracelets, necklaces, and several additional rings, however, are not. Earrings, nose rings, eyebrow rings, and other body-piercing jewelry are generally taboo. Excessive jewelry such as this is considered inappropriate. Now that the 1970s are well behind us, necklaces and bracelets in the workplace are, too. Visible tattoos are usually not acceptable in a professional environment. If you do have a tattoo, keep it covered.

The handkerchief used to be an integral part of the male wardrobe but has, in recent years, become much less popular. The two reasons for still wearing a handkerchief are for function—to use instead of tissues—and for fashion, in your coat pocket. It does provide a professional look, but be sure to fold it so that a triangle shows out of the pocket.

Another valuable accessory is a lint roller, which is a rod with a cylinder of adhesive paper on the end of it. You roll it over your clothes to pick up small pieces of lint, dirt, hair, and other undesirable debris. If you have pets, you *must* use a lint roller. Because they are so cheap, you can keep several around for your convenience.

SEWING ON BUTTONS

Another key to maintaining your wardrobe is a rudimentary knowledge of sewing. This doesn't mean you have to make your own clothes, but having the ability to sew a button back on your shirt is important. You will need a needle, about two feet of thread, and a button. You can buy these supplies cheaply at almost any store or get a free kit from most nice hotels. It's a good idea to keep a small sewing kit in your briefcase or car just to be safe.

The color of the thread should match the original color used by the manufacturer. If you cannot get a close match, use a neutral color that will not attract attention to the button.

Begin by threading the needle. Bring the two ends of the thread together and tie a triple knot. Now take the button and place it where the old button had been; there should be an indentation on the fabric. Remove the old thread with a pair of scissors.

Begin underneath the button side of the fabric, and push the needle through the fabric and into Hole A (figure 28). Pull the needle through the hole until the knot is pulled tightly against the underside of the fabric. Each time you repeat this step, be sure to pull the needle completely through to eliminate any slack in the thread. Now push the needle through Hole B and into the fabric. From the underside, pull the needle through the fabric and push up into Hole D. Next, place the needle into Hole C and push it through the fabric, remembering to pull the thread taut. This will hold the button in place and allow you to secure it for the actual sewing.

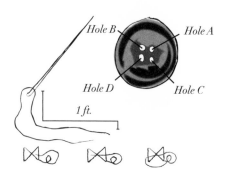

fig. 28 — The holes of a button

Now you can pull the needle through the fabric and into Hole A, then into hole B and back into the fabric. Return to Hole A and repeat the process four times. After the fourth time through Hole B, push the needle up through the fabric and into Hole D. Push the needle through Hole C, into the fabric, and back up through Hole D. Repeat this four times.

You should finish on the underside of the fabric, where you'll need to tie off the thread. To do this, pull the needle underneath the developed knot, capturing a thread or two of the fabric. As you pull it through, leave a small loop at the other side. Pull the needle back through the loop and pull the thread taut.

Repeat this with another loop. Now, simply cut the thread just above the knot. Knowing how to sew a button back on a shirt will help you easily maintain your wardrobe and save you countless trips to the tailor.

MIXING AND MATCHING

Matching is an intimidating prospect for most men. For the best results, stick to the basics unless you have great style. For those of you whose inability to match may severely limit your success, here are some basic guidelines.

The simplest approach to matching your wardrobe is having plenty of white shirts, so begin with about eight. Next, buy at least one charcoal gray and one navy blue suit and two pairs of black shoes. The key to your simple wardrobe — and to disguising the fact that it is a simple wardrobe — is owning a variety of ties. You'll need about ten, in basic designs such as paisleys, solids, simple stripes, and small patterns. Red, maroon, and yellow ties are often considered power colors, and complement both suit colors. Dark blue, royal blue, and green ties go well with gray but not with navy. Black socks are the best bet, especially if you are wearing black shoes. Never wear socks that are darker than your shoes. If you wish, you can match your socks to the dark colors in your tie. Your socks (and pants) should be long enough so that even when you cross your legs, no skin shows.

Building your wardrobe to a slightly more advanced level is not difficult. Try a gray suit with black shoes, a solid blue shirt, and a yellow tie. Another good combination is an olive suit with maroon (cordovan) shoes, a white shirt, and a multicolored tie with some olive or maroon in it. You may also consider a light gray suit, white shirt, red tie, and black shoes. These combinations will spice up your professional appearance.

BUSINESS CASUAL

Almost everyone loves casual Fridays, but what does "casual" really mean? Unfortunately, there is no universal definition. On Wall Street, it may mean a sport coat with khakis and a button down; in Austin, Texas, it usually means jeans and a golf shirt. If you are at all unsure about how casual you can be, do not risk taking a guess. Wear appropriate professional clothing on the first casual day and observe what your coworkers wear. Depending on the type of business, the weather, the city, and the standards of casual dress in your office, what is considered casual may vary greatly.

Khakis or dark dress pants are generally acceptable everywhere. With a button-down dress shirt, you can fit into almost any casual workplace. When weather permits, a golf or polo shirt may be acceptable; jeans often are not, however, so check with your coworkers before you risk it. Hats are never appropriate, nor are T-shirts or shorts. You can wear boat shoes, loafers, or even your usual dress shoes if they match the rest of your clothes. In the winter, a sweater is a good idea. Be sure to wear a collared shirt underneath the sweater, though. Remember, you do have coworkers, so do not forgo socks.

In America, a great deal of business is done on the golf course, and some companies are even paying for golf lessons for their employees. When playing golf for business, unless you are in a throwback tournament, you will not need to wear a suit to the course. Appropriate clothing for an afternoon of golf is a collared shirt with long pants or shorts, depending on the weather. Your shirt may be any color, but it should be clean and should match your pants. Usually, your best bet is khaki-colored pants or shorts. (For more golfing tips, see the Appendix on page 147.)

Some companies are now instituting "business ready" policies. Business ready is a modified form of business casual that requires you to have a jacket and tie ready, just in case a client visits or a surprise meeting is called. It is always a good idea to be ready to dress up if the circumstances demand it.

CLOTHING CHECKLIST

Here is a summary of the clothes you should have in your professional wardrobe:

If you have these items, you will have the tools to dress like a professional gentleman. Remember, high-quality clothing and accessories will help you look great with much less effort.

Items	Quantity	Description
Suits	2–6	At least one charcoal gray and one navy blue to start
Dress Shirts	12+	
White	8	Include different styles
Solid Color	2	Blue, pink
Striped	2	Blue with white stripes and maroon with white stripes
Ties	10	Professional, not "fun" ties
Dress shoes	2–3	One black pair, one brown pair
Dress belts	2	One black and one brown, or a single convertible

Items	Quantity	Description
Socks	18	10 black; 4 brown/ khaki; 4 other colors/ designs
Raincoat/ Trenchcoat	1	
Accessories		
Watch	1	High quality
Umbrellas	2	One in the car, one in the office
Quality pen	1	Names like Montblanc, Waterman, or Cross

SHAVING

There is an unwritten code at many companies that facial hair gives a bad first impression. If you choose to wear a beard or mustache, check with your colleagues to be sure that it is not frowned upon.

Assuming you do not have a beard or mustache, you must shave every day. There are no exceptions. Stubble can make you look like a teenager or a miscreant instead of a professional, no matter how well you dress.

There is a right way to shave, and unfortunately

some men just do not know how to do it. Start with a downstroke from the sideburn to the jawbone, shaving with the grain. From there, continue the downstroke from the jawline to the middle of the neck. Note that you should stop mid-neck, right around your Adam's apple.

Most men make the mistake of continuing the downstroke past the middle of the neck; the problem with this is that the grain of the hair changes and grows upward from the lower neck to mid-neck. So shave from the bottom of your neck to your Adam's apple. Next, shave straight down from your nose to your upper lip. Use sidestrokes to shave from the upper lip to the cheek.

There are several different kinds of shaving cream, but the two basic types are foamy and gel. The gel is a bit more expensive but usually provides a cleaner shave with less irritation. You might also consider one of the several types of aftershave available. Aftershave might burn a bit on contact but will seal small nicks and give you a fresh scent.

If you find that after shaving this way you still need to remove more hair, repeat the process above, this time going across, then against, the grain of your face. Realize, however, that shaving across or against the grain will further irritate your skin.

To save time and get a cleaner shave, you might consider getting a fogless mirror and shaving in the shower. It is easier to clean up and the steam from the shower helps you shave without pain.

PHYSICAL FITNESS

A discussion of professional appearance would be incomplete without at least mentioning the benefits of staying, or getting, in shape. Although there are professionals who succeed without being in shape, most truly successful businessmen spend time working out and toning their bodies. This gives them more stamina so they are able to more easily deal with consistent late hours and working under pressure. Make the time to work out: You will have more energy, and you will look like a mover and shaker.

Your professional career is predicated on your ability to deal with things like stress and pressure, long hours, and the occasional sprint through the airport to catch a flight. A good routine that includes stretching, a cardiovascular workout (running or swimming), and strength training will help you increase your stamina for those long nights at the office. When you finally get home, being in shape will also help you fall asleep faster and more soundly — not to mention you'll be more attractive in your personal life.

Pressure at the office will seem much less overwhelming if you take care of your body; somehow an overdue report isn't as daunting if you've already done a morning 5k. And then there is always the increased confidence that comes from looking your best. People often do business with those who are confident and enthusiastic. Why not use this to your advantage?

Your career does not depend on four hours a day in the gym, but by taking about one hour every other day to exercise, you can trim down, keep your heart healthy, and have more energy. After consulting with your doctor, establish a workout plan. Decide the time of day you will work out and what you will do. Allow about an hour for your workout, plus time to cool down and have a shower afterward. If you do this every other day for a month, you will see a positive change in your professional appearance.

POSTURE AND ATTITUDE

One major aspect of etiquette is demeanor, or what you say and how you act in a particular setting. In its simplest form, demeanor can include things like how you carry yourself and what kind of attitude you project. There is no question that a positive attitude is an important and fundamental aspect of etiquette; people react more favorably to individuals who smile frequently. Notice that a calm smile is called for here, not a wide, goofy grin. An easy, confident smile exudes dignity and power and is proven to relax others around you.

The way you sit, stand, and walk is also used by others as an indicator of your attitude, strength, and ability to accomplish difficult tasks. Go-getters sit up straight, stand with style, and walk tall. So, how should you carry yourself?

When sitting down, sit as if you have strings attached to your chest and shoulders. Imagine that the string is pulling your upper body so that you sit up straight. This will allow you to think more clearly, feel more energetic, and look more professional.

When standing, fight the urge to put your hands in your pockets, fold your arms, or move your hands. If you are constantly fidgeting, you will detract attention from your words. The most professional way to stand when waiting or speaking with someone is with your hands at your sides in a relaxed position. This conveys your patience, professionalism, and willingness to listen.

Walking hunched over is a big credibility robber. When you are walking, imagine that the strings attached to your chest and shoulders are now moving with you, keeping your shoulders and head straight and your chin up. Smile when you walk, even if you live in New York City. When you're crooked and grimacing, you appear angry to everyone you see, but smiling and standing up straight will improve your attitude and show others that you are a positive, self-assured person.

Part II

APPLYING FOR A JOB

WRITING A RÉSUMÉ AND COVER LETTER

A good résumé and cover letter can help you land the job of your dreams. A bad résumé and cover letter will ensure that you don't get it. First, and most important, be honest in all job application materials. Aside from the obvious moral problems involved in lying, there are numerous other reasons to tell the truth. For those of you who might be tempted to embellish your résumé, pay attention and you will quickly see why you should not.

Interviewers and human resources professionals are, by their nature, detectives. Most examine every detail with a suspicious eye and are trained to look for lies. Let's be clear: If you lie on your résumé and get caught (and that will eventually happen if you do lie), you will not get the job, or worse, you will be fired after the truth is discovered—not to mention that people will talk. When the word gets out that you are dishonest, you will lose your coworkers' respect and your career will be over. It is as simple as that. The "topgrading" method of hiring uses a specific model of interview that exposes inconsistencies and dishonesty very well. Rather than try to play games, make your life simple and just be honest.

At the same time, it is important not to be modest. Your résumé is the best, and perhaps the only, chance you'll have to "toot your own horn." Tell prospective employers the good things you have done. If you have accomplished something special, be sure to talk about it. If you were not the valedictorian, the captain of the football team, or a national merit scholar, you may think you have nothing to say, but that is rarely true. Simply look back on the past few years and find the things that you have accomplished that will make you marketable, such as any distinctions in sports, clubs and associations, volunteer activities, church groups, etc.

ORGANIZING THE RÉSUMÉ

Although there are many ways to lay out a résumé, it is simplest to set it up in the following format. Begin with your full name, centered across the top. Use a font size slightly larger than that of the body of the résumé. If you have one address, center it below your name and include your phone number and e-mail address.

If you have two addresses—for example, if you are in college and live away from home—list both, justifying each against the side columns. Include phone numbers and e-mail addresses for both.

In discussing addresses and phone numbers, here is one word of caution: Be careful about giving your current employer's address, phone number, or e-mail address to a prospective employer. Unless you are certain that your current employer will not mind that you are looking for a new job, use only your home address, phone number, and e-mail address. Also, be sure you have an answering machine or voice mail at home or on your personal cell phone. Bear in mind that your potential employer will hear your recorded greeting, so be certain that it is professional and short as described in Part V, Communication.

After you have finished adding your contact information, insert a space before moving on to the body of the résumé. On the first line of the text below the break, state your employment objective clearly and professionally. Here is an example: "To obtain full-time employment with a major public accounting firm." If your actual objective is unclear or you do not feel comfortable including one, simply leave it out. Keep in mind that you may change objectives and items on the résumé to conform to each job for which you are applying.

If you have recently graduated, the education section of your résumé should come next. If you have been in the professional world for more than a year, you might place the employment section first. Base your decision on what you think is the most relevant element of your recent past.

Depending on the last level of education you completed, you may include or exclude high school data. (If you have your PhD, high school information will probably not interest your employers.) If you are a recent college graduate, you probably want to include the name of your high school, your grade point average, any honors received, any sports played, and any activities in which you were involved. If you did well in any area, highlight it in your résumé. If you were not a star student, do not focus on academics. The smart move here is to build up your strengths and avoid your weaknesses. To the far right of this information, include the years you were in school, as well as the location of each institution.

Experience or employment history usually comes next. Here you want to focus on your accomplishments, showing the jobs you have had and how they relate to your objective, a prospective position, or your potential employer's business. Discuss your responsibilities, accomplishments, duties performed, and awards received. Show the reader that you have a variety of talents, can handle responsibility, and have been trusted in the past. Companies are much more willing to hire someone who has already proven themselves valuable as an employee. Even if your experience is at an ice cream store, you can still show that you were responsible, trustworthy, and managed people effectively.

The final section can include your hobbies, interests, and involvement in outside groups. Remember that it is up to you what you include on your résumé. It is common for applicants to have several different résumés that highlight different experiences and jobs. These résumés are tailored to particular companies and industries. If you feel that the inclusion or exclusion of any item is justified and will help a potential employer make a decision in your favor, go for it—just keep your résumé to the point. Especially if you are new to the job world, try to keep it to one page.

WRITING THE COVER LETTER

Your cover letter is very important; in many cases, it is more important than the actual résumé. Each applicant for the job will submit a résumé with his or her skills and qualifications, education, experience, and the like. Not everyone will send a cover letter, and even fewer will spend the time to properly personalize it. The goal of a cover letter is to tell the employer what benefits they will get by hiring you, and why you should be considered above all others.

Follow the same format for the cover letter as for the business letter discussed on page 138. Focus on how you will benefit the company. Tell them what makes you unique; that is, what you can do or bring to the company that no one else can. With a personalized letter that speaks directly to the company, you can allude to your résumé; but spend your time in this one-page letter convincing the reader that you are the best candidate for the job. Think of it from the employer's side. They want to hire someone who will help them prosper, financially and otherwise. Find the best way to tell them that you will help them achieve these goals, and you'll be at the top of the list. With a great cover letter and résumé, you will be in a very good position to be called in for an interview.

THE INTERVIEW

HOW TO PREPARE

When you receive an appointment for an interview with a prospective employer, learn about the company and the job for which you are applying before the interview takes place. The Internet is a great place to start, but company newsletters, annual reports, and magazine articles can also be helpful.

Try to gain a general understanding of the company, as if you were going to write a report about it. Find out who the top officers are and, if possible, uncover their personality types. Almost without exception, the leader's personality is indicative of the corporate culture. Also study current events involving the company and its industry. You can be sure that most topics in the news will be fair game for the interviewer's questions. Knowledge of current events will also give you a good base for questions to ask the interviewer.

Make sure to get a good night's rest before your interview. You want to be fresh and alert. Before you leave for the interview, do a final check to make sure you have everything that you need: a clean, crisp, comfortable suit that is free of lint and spots; at least five copies of your résumé; your portfolio and pen; and a positive attitude!

WHAT TO DISCUSS

Arrive a few minutes early—but be prepared to sit in a coffee shop or in your car if you're more than ten minutes early. You might be imposing on the office if you show up too soon and the staff is busy on other tasks—don't expect the interviewer to see you before your appointed time. Once the interview starts, begin to build a rapport by sitting up straight, smiling, and looking directly into the person's eyes when you speak. During the first few minutes, the interviewer will create his or her basic impression of you, which will quite possibly directly affect your chances of getting hired. Often the interview will begin with a discussion of your résumé or an employment form designed by the company. Reviewing this familiar information will help you relax.

As discussed in the résumé section, you must be honest. Lying will only make you uncomfortable.

You need to be relaxed to freely discuss your accomplishments. Be modest but positive about your experiences and be sure you are able to explain how you overcame problems or hurdles in your life. Most interviewers now ask you for a situation in which you dealt with difficulty or failure, and what you learned in the process.

If you were previously employed, the interviewer will almost always ask about your former employer. Do not take this as an invitation to complain about how horrible your experience was or how much you hate your old boss, even if it is true. This question is designed to evaluate what kind of relationship you had with your previous employer. Be honest, but do not say that your boss hated you or that you hated him or her. Try to mention the benefits of working at the job and talk about things you learned that will help you in your next position.

Candidates often fear the difficult questions that they may have to answer. In general, if you are faced with a question that you cannot solve, do not guess or make up an answer. It is much easier to say, "I don't know, but I will find out and call you with the answer tomorrow." You will appear much more intelligent and honest, and you will not have to be afraid of the truth.

CONCERNS AND OBSTACLES IN THE INTERVIEW

You may face some minor obstacles during your interview. The worst is the question that seems off the wall. He or she may call it a "probing" or "character" question—they're supposed to give the interviewer an insight into what kind of person you are. An example is, "If you could be any kind of fruit, what kind would you be?" If you are asked a question like this, do your best to answer it, but don't get stressed; there is no "right" answer.

Your interviewer may also ask a question that will test your analytical and problem-solving abilities. It could be a system question or a riddle. A system question tests your problem-solving methods. For example, let's say your interviewer asks, "How many gas stations are there in the United States?" He or she is interested not in the exact amount of gas sold. Rather, the interviewer is trying to discover how you arrive at your answer. These questions will test your assumptions and mathematical calculations for logic but not necessarily numerical accuracy.

Answer this type of question by taking time to think it through logically. Count the number of gas stations in your town. Now estimate the population in your town. Divide the population by that of the

United States. Using ratios, now divide the number of stations by the percentage of your town's population and you will have a rough but good answer.

Another interview technique is the riddle. Here the interviewer asks you a complex riddle that requires you to think "outside the box." This could be something like the riddle about the farmer getting his chicken, fox, and grain across the river or it could be a curveball question like "Why are manholes round?" Knowing how to answer these questions in the moment can be very helpful. There are several good books on riddles that will give you some samples and some tips on solving new problems.

Another idea is to talk to others who have recently interviewed with the company and ask them for some pointers. Since each company is different, it helps to have some insight before you get there.

DINING DURING AN INTERVIEW

During the interview process, you may be invited to a lunch either as part of a full day of interviews or just for a "relaxed" setting. Do not be fooled; this setting is no more relaxing than being in an office. It does, however, give the employer a great chance to see you outside the office, and it serves as a window to the "true you." You will be under the microscope throughout the entire interview, even at lunch. Watch how you treat others, especially the staff at the restaurant.

You might think that because the interviewer is going to pick up the check (and he or she will), you can order anything you want. This is not, however, an invitation for you to order the most expensive item on the menu. Choose a meal with a moderate price and one that is easy to eat. That basically means avoiding finger foods and pasta dishes, which can really make a mess. You want the interviewer to focus on your ability to work well, not on the huge bill and the sauce on your shirt.

A test that interviewers for large companies used in the 1970s was called "the Salt Test." They would check to see if the candidate would salt or pepper his or her food before tasting it. They surmised that anyone who would salt their food before tasting it was too quick to judge and thus was not executive material. Although this may seem like an odd test, some interviewers still use it. So, even if you love your salt or pepper, make sure you taste your food first. It's pretty easy to do, and it could save you from making a huge mistake.

ASKING QUESTIONS

At the end of every interview, you will be given an opportunity to ask questions. *Use it*. Find out what you want to know but have not been able to learn from your initial research. Having said that, there is such a thing as a stupid question in an interview situation. These can include asking how much money the position pays, what the vacation policy is, what the company does, and what your chances of getting the job are. Make a point to ask something that will help you to be chosen over other candidates. Ask about a "day in the life" of the person currently in the position for which you are applying or how the company can offer you growth, both personally and professionally. Depending on the interviewer's perceived openness to suggestions, you might want to use your earlier research on the company to make a suggestion for a new opportunity they might consider. Many companies would appreciate this display of initiative.

AFTER THE INTERVIEW

After the interview, be sure to follow up with a thank-you letter to the interviewer or interviewers. This can take the form of a card or letter—but not an e-mail. The most important part is to thank the individual for his or her time and consideration. You may also answer questions you were unable to answer during the interview, provide other information, or ask another question. Be sure to personalize the communication by making a reference to your interview. If you met with more than one person, be sure to send a separate thank-you letter to each and mail them in separate envelopes. Be sure to send your thank-you note as soon as you get home, preferably on the day of the interview.

Part III

OFFICE ETIQUETTE

YOUR BEHAVIOR DICTATES YOUR SUCCESS

Now that you've landed the job, the focus often shifts from etiquette to your actual work product. Don't fall into the trap of thinking that proper behavior doesn't matter anymore. The way you act and treat others will not only affect how your colleagues treat you, but also your chances for advancement.

BEING ON TIME

Not everyone finds it easy to be punctual. Most people who call when they say they will and arrive on time have to work at it. Professionals must become masters of time. Making a point of being exactly on time is an obvious way of showing your attention to detail, and people who are known for punctuality are well respected and trusted.

When arriving for a meeting, show up about one minute before the scheduled time. You do not want to rush someone by showing up too early. On the other hand, being late shows a lack of consideration. If you become unavoidably detained, call the person or people you are meeting with as soon as possible. Realize, however, that you should make every effort to be on time. The first time you plan to meet someone at an unfamiliar location—or if you are concerned about being late—plan on arriving fifteen to twenty minutes early. You can use this extra time in your car or outside the building to deal with small administrative tasks such as catching up on phone calls or reading.

ORGANIZATION AND TIME MANAGEMENT

Staying organized is a huge part of being successful in business. Although a clean and organized desk will not guarantee a promotion, it will definitely help you find materials and complete tasks quickly. Work to keep your office or cubicle clean; clients and superiors will be put off by a messy workspace. Institute a good filing system that incorporates hanging folders or other organizational tools. Don't be afraid to rid your desk of papers that will not serve you in the future. Your trashcan should be your most-used filing device.

Planning is the key to time management, so get a good daily planner or application for your handheld device. Many different styles are available; as long as you actually use the planner, the type doesn't matter. Make sure that it allows you to plan on a daily, weekly, monthly, and long-term basis. It should also have room for names, addresses, and phone numbers.

Many professionals supplement their planners by including a to-do list with the major items for the day, in order of importance. You can either do this in the pages of your planner or on a separate sheet that you can replace as you see fit. You might also choose to keep your key names and addresses in the planner on sheets printed out from your computer. The idea is to include as much helpful and useful information in your planner as possible. When you need to contact someone, it is a wonderful feeling to know, beyond a shadow of a doubt, that you have his or her information in your planner or mobile device.

SHAKING HANDS

All it takes is three seconds, but the handshake is an important component in that very powerful first impression. The moment you are introduced to someone, usually when the person you're meeting is a few feet away from you, extend your right hand. You should find a happy medium in the strength of your grip: A firm handshake is best, but don't injure the person you are meeting. You want the person you are meeting to know that you are a solid person who can be trusted and counted on.

Your fingers should be relatively close to each other but not actually touching, and your thumb should be pointed straight up. As your hand meets the other hand, make sure that you touch your thumb-finger web to that of the other person. Next, place your thumb on his or her hand, and squeeze the hand as if you were squeezing the ketchup out of a plastic container. As you shake the hand, square your shoulders to the person. Smile and look him or her in the eye. You should shake for about three pumps, then slowly pull your hand away.

If you are at an occasion that requires a name tag, be sure to place it on your right breast pocket to make it easier for others to read as they shake your hand. At a cocktail party, keep your drink in your left hand. Since you will shake with your right hand, you do not want it to be cold and wet from the glass. If you shake someone's hand and find it wet, cold, or sweaty, do not draw attention to the condition, even in a joking manner. Act as if were completely normal and move on. By politely ignoring it, you will help the other person feel more comfortable with you.

Some people are unable to shake with their right hand because of a disability. They are probably used to shaking with their left hand or greeting in some other way. The best advice is to watch them and follow their lead. If they offer to shake with their left hand or approach your left side, extend your left hand. If they go for your right, they will cup their left hand on top of yours.

You'll also want to remember that if there is a health scare or outbreak of a particular disease going on, some people may be reluctant to shake hands. Some (including Donald Trump) refuse to shake hands at all. While this is pretty uncommon, respect other person's wishes and refrain from the handshake.

As odd as it sounds, you should practice shaking hands with family members or friends. A good handshake will help you present a strong first impression and illustrate your attention to detail in even the most common aspects of human interaction.

EXCHANGING BUSINESS CARDS

A business card is key to establishing yourself in the professional world. Hand them out to your friends, family, new and old acquaintances, and anyone else who you think may help you. Also remember to ask for others' cards and save them; building a large file of cards can really pay off in the future. Keep in mind, however, that it is usually inappropriate for a junior person to ask a senior person for a card. Feel free to give your card in return, but make sure your superior initiates the process.

When you get a card, jot a few notes on the back — how you met the person, the issues you discussed, and personal information that you have in common. Keep the cards in a centralized location or invest in a scanner that can digitize the cards so you can put them into contact management software. Contact the card owners at least once a year to keep the lines of communication open. Many people send a holiday card to everyone on their list; this marginal cost can help to build your professional image and create a powerful personal network.

CANCELING MEETINGS

Although canceling meetings is somewhat common, you should not do it lightly. A meeting, by definition, involves more than one person; if you have to cancel, you'll be affecting at least one other person's schedule. Before scrapping the meeting entirely, consider the chance that someone else can go in your stead or that the others can still meet and accomplish some of the planned objectives. If neither of these alternatives is appropriate, call the other person (or people) as soon as you are certain the meeting cannot take place and offer a suggestion that will work instead. It might be a teleconference, a web-based live chat, or another meeting at a different time, but put forth some alternatives before canceling the meeting altogether. Realize also that you have made other people's schedules more complicated, so be considerate and willing to compromise your schedule a bit for their convenience.

USING SICK DAYS AND VACATION DAYS

We all get sick. We all need vacations. However, most employees don't know the best ways to use these days off. The first thing you should do is become familiar with your company's policy. Many companies group sick days and vacation days into a "PTO" (paid time off) account. Other companies have a set amount of time for both sick days and vacation days. Still more companies offer a "mental health" day each month. Be sure you know what kind of day you are taking before you call in to notify your boss.

If you are sick and you think that your illness is contagious, take the day off. Your coworkers do not want you to infect them, and your body needs the downtime. Most illnesses can be cured in a day or two if you allow yourself enough rest. Be sure you know ahead of time the name of the person you should notify about your absence, his or her extension, and when to place the call. You will probably need to call as early as possible in order to give your team enough time to plan their day around your absence.

Most companies have set guidelines for when and how you can take vacation days. For example, most accounting firms are usually unwilling to allow vacations from the beginning of the year through April 15. Other companies require employees to give six weeks' notice before taking vacation days. So be sure to check before you make any plans that you wouldn't want to break. If no formal structures are in place, give a reasonable amount of notice — at least two weeks — so that company plans can be changed if need be. If you consider the needs of your employer when taking sick days and requesting vacation time, you will avoid creating problems and inconveniences—and you'll also keep your sanity!

BUSINESS TRAVEL

Corporate meetings and trade conferences in various parts of the country may make flying a necessity for many professionals. Although flying etiquette is rather simple, it is certainly important enough to be covered here. Traveling with courtesy and foresight can prevent many undesirable situations and enhance your status as a true gentleman.

Pack lightly and sensibly. Make sure to include the essentials, but do not overburden yourself with too many accessories or unnecessary items. You may want to call your hotel to see if your room will be equipped with a blow dryer, iron, and ironing board. If the hotel provides these important items, you can save yourself a lot of packing space. Whenever possible, bring only one carry-on suitcase and keep it small enough to fit below the seat in front of you. In it, include reading material, a complete change of attire, a razor, and a toothbrush. Delays can happen when you least expect them, and it's usually at the most inopportune time. It's always better to prepare yourself by carrying an extra change of clothes—just in case.

When you reach your seat, realize that most passengers are interested in their reading or other personal matters. They would probably prefer not to talk to you, even if you are charming and entertaining. Bring some reading material, usually more than you think you'll need. If you're delayed, you'd much rather be reading something of your choice than the latest SkyMall catalog.

Here are a few more tips for the frequent traveler:

- Join all the frequent flyer/traveler programs you can for every airline, hotel, and car-rental company. They're free and can quickly earn free travel perks.

- Pick a favorite airline and hotel and try to travel them the most. Each group has a top tier of benefits that get better the more you travel.

- Try to sit in exit rows. They have a little more legroom and are usually free of small children.

- Remember that alcohol affects you more at higher altitudes, so limit the number of cocktails you order.

If you fly a particular airline often, consider joining one of the pay clubs, which offer a more relaxed setting, office equipment, and some amenities that the average traveler doesn't get.

BATHROOM ETIQUETTE

Few things are more personal than trips to the bathroom, yet no discussion of etiquette is complete without addressing this topic, which seems to escape many men.

Let's assume we're talking about a bathroom with more than one toilet or urinal. There are a few basic rules. First, don't try to make new friends. If you don't know someone in the bathroom, don't start talking to them there. Networking is a big part of modern life, but the bathroom should be kept a sanctuary.

Second, there are some basic rules for using a row of urinals. When you're standing, look forward, even if the wall in front of you is boring. Looking at your neighbors on your sides is rude and might get you punched. Remember, this isn't a social visit. Don't strike up a conversation, and avoid sound effects—this was funny when we were in grade school but that time has long passed. Also, whenever possible, allow a one urinal buffer between you and others.

Third, wash your hands. It's a sad comment on our times that any public bathroom where food is served has to have a sign requiring employees to wash their hands, but studies have shown that about one-third of Americans don't wash their hands after using the restroom. This is not only gross, but it can also hurt your reputation if others see that you don't wash your hands. Get in the habit of always washing, even if you don't pee on your hands.

Finally, people are pretty conscious of germs and often don't like to open a door knowing that most people who open it don't wash. Grab a paper towel and use it to open the door. Also, be aware of others around you, and if someone is leaving, hold the door for them too. You can discard the paper towel outside the restroom if there isn't a trash right near the door.

MISCELLANEOUS OFFICE ETIQUETTE TIPS

Here are a few other useful office etiquette tips:

- If you have a kitchen or coffee station in your office, do not be afraid to make coffee, but always clean up after yourself. Spend an extra three minutes cleaning up a mess or washing a dish or two, and you will generate an amazing amount of goodwill.

- When walking with coworkers, be courteous. If you walk slowly or quickly, adjust your speed to accommodate the others in your group.

- If you feel a sneeze coming on, use your left hand and a tissue to cover your nose and mouth. This keeps your right hand clean so that, if need be, you can shake hands later.

- Part of keeping up your image is staying fiscally responsible. At one extreme, this means avoiding personal bankruptcy. At the other extreme, it means being conscious of not flaunting your wealth. Money can be a wonderful tool in life, but it should not be your ultimate goal.

RESIGNING FROM A JOB

If you're leaving your present employer, I hope it's because you've just taken a great job offer from a super company. But no matter the reason, sometimes you have to resign from a position. Although some companies have stringent rules on how to terminate employment, most rules are not as strict. The best way to leave a company is to show respect for your employer's business and your coworkers. This means that you should give them a reasonable amount of time (at least two weeks) to find a replacement and to have you train that person before you go. Although you might have been treated poorly at this job, resist the urge to get back at your old employer. Do not take office supplies, ruin client relationships, or make the transition difficult. Word gets around in the business community; don't say or do anything that you wouldn't want your next employer to hear about. Most people will not tolerate unprofessional behavior, even if you think it's warranted. Besides, burning bridges is not a good business decision— you never know when your paths might cross again. Your best bet is to be happy (and perhaps relieved) that you'll be working at a new job soon.

Part IV

PERSONAL
INTERACTION

CHIVALRY: THE BEGINNING

Chivalry, still considered a noble concept, is the parent of modern etiquette. Many of the customs embodied in proper etiquette were born in the chivalric code of the Middle Ages.

Those who say that chivalry is dead are wrong. Those who say that chivalry is male chauvinism are also wrong. A true gentleman treats both men and women with respect and is willing to help anyone in need. While there may be a few people who do not appreciate an act of chivalry, no man is ever faulted for treating others with respect and dignity.

So, how does one learn the rules of chivalry? The governing principle is that a busy person can take a few extra seconds out of his day to help make other people's lives easier. Treat others as if they are the most important people in the world, even if you are more interested in other things. Many of the rules of chivalry are quite basic and are probably already part of your subconscious thought. If not, you might want to practice them until they become ingrained.

For example, when you get to a door first, hold it open for others before you enter. After you have gone through the door, look to see if you could hold it for someone else. It might take an extra five to six seconds, but you will garner respect and hone your etiquette skills in the process.

When entering an elevator, wait for all people who are exiting that floor to leave and hold the door for anyone who might be waiting. Then you may enter the elevator. If there is enough room in the car, stand to the side; do not invade anyone's personal space. Also remember that it is rude to force others in the car to listen to your conversations, whether you are on a cell phone or chatting with another person in the elevator. If you are traveling with a coworker, be especially careful to avoid discussing confidential information; you have no idea who might be listening. When you reach your floor, hold the door from the inside for anyone who is leaving and, once you exit, for anyone who wants to get into the elevator.

When guests are visiting your office or home, offer to take their coats and ask if they would like a drink. If you show them to another room, hold the door and wait for the group to enter before you do. Take care of your guests and they will notice your attention to detail and etiquette. Similarly, when at a restaurant with a client, coworker, or friend, offer to take the other person's coat. Once you arrive at the table, offer to push the chair in if a woman needs assistance. Of course women can do this for themselves, but your offer shows that you know how to treat others properly.

When you are walking down the street with a woman, take the outside position, closest to the traffic, a move considered old-fashioned but extremely classy. This rule started back in the era of packed-dirt streets, horse-drawn carriages, and flowing dresses. When the rain soaked the streets, a thick layer of mud would form. Passing carriages would then splatter the mud onto the pedestrians. In an effort to spare the ladies the expense of cleaning their many-layered dresses, the gentlemen would walk on the outside to guard the ladies from splashing mud.

Although the pragmatism of the man walking on the outside is considerably lessened in the era of paved streets, any observant person, including women who are aware of this tradition, will see the gentlemanly nature of your acts and be impressed that you know how to treat people properly. When you get to a car, open the door for others first, and then you may enter. Remember that the most senior person should sit in the most comfortable seat, usually in the front. It is a good rule to be the last one in the car, especially if you are driving. If you have any control over the radio, seriously consider keeping it off. Unless you are certain that everyone enjoys your taste in music, you should try to eliminate forcing your music on other passengers. If music is desired by your passengers, allow them to pick the station. When using public transportation, offer your seat to a woman or elderly person; they might not accept, but it is a kind and gentlemanly gesture.

A brief discussion of sexual harassment is integral to any etiquette book, and a section on chivalry and respect for others seems to be the perfect place for it. In the past twenty years, society has finally begun to recognize the dangers of sexual harassment. As a general rule, avoid all questionable behavior and material in the workplace. Your personal life is your own—but as soon as you assume working responsibilities, you are under the microscope. If anyone can perceive your behavior as sexual harassment, you are in trouble. At the office, avoid jokes, e-mail, and conversation that can be construed as sexual. You may miss out on a laugh or two, but the risk of a sexual harassment suit is just not worth it.

The concepts of chivalry and gender equality are not mutually exclusive. A true gentleman knows that by being chivalrous he is simply being kind and considerate; he is not asserting his dominance. Following the basics of chivalry will complement the more detailed elements of modern business etiquette.

PERSONAL BASICS

You display your etiquette skills in the way you treat and interact with every person you meet, from the CEO to the most junior assistant. Thus, the second building block in your etiquette development is the basics of personal interaction. Following my school motto—Responsibility, Loyalty, and Consideration— will help guide you in your relationships with friends, coworkers, and anyone else in your life.

RESPONSIBILITY

It seems that in today's culture, responsibility has become an antiquated notion. Many people are unwilling to take responsibility for negative situations and instead prefer to call themselves victims. This "victim-itis" is common in professional circles and plays a big part in office politics. Fight this disease with all your might; when you are given a task, take responsibility for your actions. If you succeed, that's wonderful; be sure to give credit to everyone who helped you. If you do not, learn from it, and take full responsibility for the error. Although this might seem to be a game plan that will get you fired quickly, it will in fact do the opposite. Your coworkers, subordinates, and superiors will respect you as one of the few people in the professional arena who takes responsibility for his actions. It is also the right thing to do, and doing what is right is a fundamental part of etiquette. If you work in an office where honesty and responsibility get you fired, then look for new work. It's not worth working for an employer unwilling to allow mistakes.

LOYALTY

Loyalty is another trait that is often dismissed in our culture. Loyalty to your company, your boss, your coworkers, and your subordinates is integral in building strong interpersonal relationships — although, to be clear, I am not recommending blind loyalty. When you are trusted with information and tasks, fulfill your duty with dedication and honesty and you will reap the rewards. If you are disloyal, on the other hand, you will ruin your reputation. Then, no matter how sharply you dress or how good your table manners are, you will never be respected.

Remember that after Benedict Arnold defected to the British during the Revolutionary War, the English commanders never trusted him with a battle command because of his earlier disloyalty. No one remembers all his achievements for the United States before he became a traitor. If you are disloyal, no one — not even those you help — will be able to trust you.

CONSIDERATION

Consideration in the form of empathy — but not necessarily sympathy — is a large part of etiquette. Being considerate of others shows that you will attempt to understand situations before making snap judgments. Given the option, people will almost always work with someone who is open and thoughtful rather than rash and impulsive.

These three traits—responsibility, loyalty, and consideration—will help guide you in your relationships and implement the basics of etiquette in your life.

THE PLATINUM RULE®

Every company, family, or group of any kind has at least one person who is friendly with everyone. You know the type; he or she is always smiling, is nice to everyone, and seems to be everyone's friend. These people find success because they make others feel comfortable. They realize that no matter the minor differences of wealth, class, intelligence, or background, all people are worthy of respect.

My friend Dr. Tony Alessandra has developed a rule to describe people who have a special knowledge of others—he calls them masters of "The Platinum Rule." (You can learn more about it at www.platinumrule.com.) The Golden Rule, which you were probably taught in kindergarten, states that one should treat others as one would like to be treated him- or herself. Taking a new approach to this truth, The Platinum Rule says that one should treat others the way *they* want to be treated. Those who are skilled in etiquette employ The Platinum Rule by paying attention to the needs and desires of others at all times.

Most people are not cryptic. They let you know what they like and how they want to be treated. While some people are very serious in the workplace, others laugh all day long. By following The Platinum Rule, you can be serious with those who prefer to be serious and more jovial with those who are more relaxed. Your job, as someone who works to embody etiquette, is to pay attention and treat people the way they want to be treated. The Platinum Rule will allow you to make others feel comfortable in your presence and prompt them to treat you well in turn.

OFFICE POLITICS

"People will talk." You have heard it before, and it is nowhere more true than in the workplace. If you haven't already worked in an office, you will find that when you do, office politics and the proverbial grapevine not only exist but often run rampant. You must be prepared for this; expect it and accept it.

This does not mean, however, that you have to play the game. It is very easy to sit with your coworkers and complain about your boss, other coworkers, or subordinates, but it is not in good taste. Simply put: Do not do it. There is no good reason to sit in on these discussions, let alone participate in them. The information—or misinformation—is harmful not only to the subjects of the discussion but to the speaker and the listener as well. By participating, you often help spread faulty information. Also, if you tell others how you dislike someone with whom you are usually pleasant, they will realize that they cannot trust what you say. Rise above the gossip. Stick to your work and the tasks that will help you succeed. You will be stronger and more respected for it in the end.

When you work to develop a friendly rapport with your coworkers, be smart about it. A proven plan is to be respectful with everyone and give possible friendships plenty of time to develop. People respond well when they are treated with respect. Most office friendships are best developed slowly. If you make your coworkers feel comfortable by treating them with respect, you will build strong relationships naturally over time.

When you are first getting to know your new coworkers, be wary of constantly going out with them. A drink or two after work is usually a good way to start out, but keep it to one or two. The key to after-hours socialization is to limit its time and extent; learn the fine art of leaving people wanting more. Becoming too friendly too soon often results in awkward relationships that may turn ugly. There are several benefits to getting to know your fellow workers outside of the office; just remember to give the relationships time to develop. Dating in the office should also be approached with extreme care; this is covered more deeply on page 106.

When you're in the office, or even in an after-hours social setting, act as if your every action is being recorded. This may seem cynical, but it is the safest course to follow. Refrain from making lewd jokes, as they will almost certainly offend someone. Never mock or imitate anyone; this type of behavior is cruel and rude. It often gets back to the person you are imitating and will definitely harm you. Even if you think you are funny, you are still out of line.

The exponential increase in sexual harassment cases proves that any touching, of either men or women, is inappropriate in the professional environment. Although it may be somewhat awkward, avoid physical contact with your coworkers in the office. This will demonstrate both your professionalism and your respect for each person's "personal space." Remember, if you treat everyone with respect, you will build strong relationships with your coworkers.

DATING IN THE OFFICE

Dating in the office is usually frowned on, but in the real world, it happens. When you spend hours each day with someone, if there is some sort of romantic spark, it will often catch fire. So what do you do? The first step is to consider company policies. Most companies discourage romance between employees at different levels because of the perceived impropriety. Be sure that your company does not explicitly prohibit dating. After reviewing the risks and company policies, if you still decide to continue the relationship, do your best to keep the personal side separate from the business side. There is no excuse for spending time at work on your love life. Realize as well that if the relationship leads to something serious like marriage, the company might request that one or both of you transfer—or even resign—to avoid the appearance of impropriety.

SOCIAL NETWORKING

In the new world of social networking, it's important to remember that just about everything that goes on the web will be there—*forever*. That means pictures of you doing silly/stupid things, even years ago, may come back to haunt you. Specific thoughts or ideas that you express may offend others. Rude, incorrect, or mean-spirited statements you make about others will most likely become part of the permanent Internet archive and can only hurt you. A gentleman never uses social networking tools for negative or hurtful comments, and he also knows that paying attention to his past and avoiding questionable pictures and statements online will protect him from embarrassment—or worse—in the future.

CONVERSING ABOUT CURRENT EVENTS

There is an obvious need to stay informed about the current events that affect your company, profession, and industry. If your biggest competitor files for bankruptcy, it is important for you to have a basic knowledge about what happened and what the impact might be on you and your company.

There are many things you can learn by keeping up to date with current events. But more importantly, it is imperative to be able to speak intelligently with your coworkers—people are often judged by their ability to engage in small talk. The Internet is full of sites that provide quick and clear news to help you stay informed. Follow news sites as well as industry-specific sites.

Most professionals need to have at least a rudimentary knowledge of the issues facing the world today. The reason is that in many of the relaxed professional settings where small talk is prevalent, the discussion often turns to current events. It is quite embarrassing when your boss asks you a question about your thoughts on a political or economic issue, and you have no idea what the issue is, let alone what you think of it.

Remember that current events will come up in daily conversation, and it pays to have some knowledge about them. You are constantly being judged; by keeping up to date, you can make a good impression—even during small talk.

INTERACTING WITH SUPPORT STAFF

It is a mistake to think that you can get away with

ignoring or treating support or administrative staff poorly. Proper etiquette requires you to treat everyone with respect and dignity. Breach this code and you will suffer. Professionals know that their successes are based on the quality of their staff at all levels and rely on them heavily. A good manager is aware of who treats his or her people properly and who does not, and many managers will take it personally if their staff is treated poorly; it will be as if you had been rude to the manager directly.

You will find that asking people for favors is a much more fruitful endeavor if you have always treated them with dignity. If you need a colleague or administrative employee to work late, or someone in the mailroom to rush an overnight package to the airport, keep in mind that they will remember how you have treated them (and their colleagues) in the past. This sort of word, good or bad, spreads quickly. Don't expect to get away with treating your boss well and other staff members poorly; you will be exposed quickly, and then neither group will trust you.

When a member of administrative staff successfully completes a task, take the time to praise the individual in public for his or her effort. One of the best traits you can develop is to effectively praise subordinates for a job well done. You don't have to throw a party in the person's honor for every achievement; sometimes a simple memo or genuine thank-you will do.

A client's staff can be a huge help to you as well. If you have a good relationship with a client's assistant, you can count on extra help when you need it. This also goes for prospects—that is, those with whom you want to do business in the future. If you call on someone who is interested in doing business with your company, he or she will almost always ask the receptionist how you behaved while you were waiting and how you spoke and acted. It's a great help to have an extra cheerleader in your camp, so remember to respect everyone.

Never underestimate the number of times you will have to call a client needing to speak about an important issue and be at the mercy of his or her staff. If you have a good relationship with the staff, many more doors will open and more opportunities will become available. Before your first visit to the client, it's usually a good idea to call ahead and get a feel for the office culture and dress code. Check with the person who answers the phone to see whether you should wear business casual or a suit, or if jeans are dressy enough.

This is an important rule to keep in mind when interviewing at prospective employers as well. A "greeter" will often take your coat and make you comfortable while you wait. This person will also answer any questions you have before the interview process starts. The greeter will usually be younger than you and will act like a friend, but never doubt that everything you say and do will be reported back to the person making the hiring decision. Treat the greeter with respect and you will benefit immensely; act irresponsibly and you will suffer.

BUSINESS DINING

Any discussion of professional conduct would be incomplete without a discussion of table manners, especially since many business meetings involve a meal. As with any other type of etiquette, good table manners may not explicitly help you, but bad table manners will definitely hurt you.

To get your bearings, see the illustration of a typical table setting in figure 29. The simplest rule for using silverware is to work from the outside in, toward the plate, as the meal progresses. Your forks are on the left. If there are two of them, the smaller outer fork is the salad fork, and the larger inner one is the dinner fork. On the right, from the outside in, are the spoon and the knife. The blade of the knife will be facing toward the plate. If there is a large spoon and a small spoon, the smaller is the fruit spoon and the larger is the soup spoon. A spoon or fork found above your plate is for dessert, and your beverage and coffee cup will be located on the upper right corner of your table setting. The salad plate will be on your left side with your bread plate.

fig. 29 — A typical table setting

As soon as you sit down at the table, find your napkin, unfold it, and put it on your lap. Leave your nondominant hand on your lap or on the edge of the table and keep it there for most of the meal. You will want to eat with your dominant hand. The only time you will use both hands is when you are cutting your food. To cut properly, hold your fork upside down with your nondominant hand and your knife with your dominant hand. As soon as you have finished cutting, place the knife back on the right side of the plate or across the top of the plate, and switch your fork to your dominant hand to eat.

When eating bread, break off a small piece, butter it, and eat it. Do not butter the whole piece of bread or roll all at once. Similarly, do not cut your food into many pieces at the beginning of the meal. Simply cut off the piece you will eat, chew it well, and then cut again. Use your napkin often to clean any crumbs from your lips. When someone asks you to pass the salt or pepper, pass both shakers at the same time. Never reach across anyone's "personal space" when taking an item for your own use or passing an item to someone else; simply ask the person next to you to pass the item for you.

If you get up during the meal, place the napkin on your chair. This lets the waitstaff know that you will be returning soon. When you finish with a spoon,

place it on the saucer under your soup dish or coffee cup, not in the bowl or cup itself. As soon as you
have finished your meal, place your knife across the
top of the plate, with the blade facing you. Next, place
your fork and other used utensils closer to the middle of the plate and parallel to the knife. The fork's
tines should be facing down. Finally, fold your napkin
loosely and place it on the table (figure 30). If you
follow these simple rules, you will greatly lessen the
chances of committing a serious faux pas at a business meal.

fig. 30—Placement of used utensils and napkin

Paying for meals is often a confusing element of
etiquette, but there are generally accepted rules you
can follow. First, when you are being interviewed

for a job or your boss is taking you out for a perfor-mance review, you can expect them to pay for the meal. The most basic rule is that the person who invites the other for the meal usually pays for it. However, if there is ever a question, always be willing to take the whole bill yourself and treat the others to a nice meal. By paying most of the time, you gain two advantages over those with whom you eat — the other person will often feel somewhat indebted to you, and you eliminate the awkwardness of waiting for someone to pick up the tab. If another person buys, be sure to give genuine thanks.

When eating with clients, you should generally plan to pay for the meal. If they do take the bill, be sure to get it next time and at least alternate paying — but avoid letting your clients pay for too many meals. I'm also a big fan of treating my vendors to meals. Vendors usually have to pay for client meals and are surprised when you pick up the tab. You'll often find that they return the favor with great information or lower prices in the future.

Usually, you will not be eating with your superi-ors on a regular basis, so it is acceptable for them to pay for the meal. But if you do eat with them often, you should expect to pay for yourself most of the time. One caveat is that if you invite the superior to a restaurant for a special purpose, such as to ask for a special raise or promotion, you should offer to pay.

You will probably not eat with your subordinates very often either. Make a point to pay for their meals some of the time, but do not pay every time, as they may begin to expect it. When eating with those at your level, you should usually pay your own way, but pick up the check every once in a while for a nice treat.

When you invite someone to eat, you are making a big impression. Unfortunately, the invitation alone does not necessarily mean it will be a good impression. The best way to prepare yourself for good impressions is to build relationships with local restaurants near your office and around town. Pick three or four that serve a variety of foods, and one or two with a special theme or menu. (It's a good idea to know a place for people with dietary restrictions, a place for vegans, and a place with local flair.)

You should make a point to visit these places at least once a month. Tip very well (25–30 percent) and be friendly with the host or hostess and servers. After a few visits, ask them to give you an account. They can either bill you at the end of each month or keep your credit card on file and charge all your meals to it. Either way, be sure that many of the servers know who you are and treat you with respect. This relationship allows you to focus on the business at hand, knowing that you will have great service and that the bill is not an issue. Once you have a relationship with a restaurant, you will be able to get a great table on short notice, you will not have to wait to be seated, and the service will be excellent.

With these relationships firmly in place, you will have more flexibility when making plans with your clients. Ask them where they will be before you plan to eat and cater the invitation to your client's location. This will also give you a bit of an edge with the client, since you will be in a comfortable environment during the meal. The question of paying for the meal will be answered as soon as you sit at your table, your drink will be waiting for you, and the staff will address you by name. Your clients will most likely notice your good rapport with the staff and your excellent attention to detail in choosing and dining at restaurants.

You'll also need to know how to tip appropriately at the end of the meal, and there are many schools of thought when it comes to tipping. In Europe, people usually just round up to the nearest round number. In the US, a standard tip for a meal is 15 percent; for valets and bellmen, a few dollars is usually standard. I have a different opinion on this. I tend to overtip, and I do it on purpose. I like to say thanks to people who provide me good service—not just because it's polite, but also because if I give them a little more, they are more apt to help me in the future. Since I never know when I'll see someone again, I like to leave them with a good impression. Pick a tipping plan that is comfortable for you, but my experience says that you'll rarely be upset that you overtipped, and will often be delighted with the great service that comes from it.

Part V

COMMUNICATION

HUMOR

While business is often serious, there is no harm in having a healthy sense of humor. Some companies are known for the fun they have, and they reap many benefits as a result of that fun. There are many different kinds of humor, from a dry wit to a more biting style. Although some biting comments may be funny or even accurate, be sure you are not laughing or making jokes at another's expense. There is no exception to this rule, even if the person you are insulting is not going to find out about your joke. Also, it's best to avoid sarcasm completely.

So, how can you show humor in the workplace? Self-effacing humor is a fantastic way to make jokes while showing that you are confident and able to poke fun at yourself. An added benefit of this type of humor is that if you make a mistake and then make light of your folly, it is much more difficult for others to hold you in contempt for the error. Your confidence will impress them. By making the joke, you are admitting that you messed up, showing that it is not the end of the world, and encouraging others to admit mistakes openly.

LANGUAGE

The language you use in the professional world is important. An extensive vocabulary can quickly illustrate your intelligence and creativity. At the same time, there is rarely an excuse for swearing in the office. It might seem cool and part of being a big shot, but gentlemen do not swear in the workplace. The extensive use of four-letter words shows an inability to fully learn the English language and is characteristic of someone who is inconsiderate to his coworkers and clients. (I'm sometimes guilty of this and have, unfortunately, offended people unnecessarily. Take it from me, it's really embarrassing.) If you must express your disdain, show your intelligence and creativity and use more descriptive words.

One way to do this is to watch cartoons and movies geared toward children. Listen to the ways super-villains express their anger and pick your favorite. Some of the better ones are "rats," "blast," and "gadzooks!" It is your responsibility to contain your anger and limit your use of expletives.

If you can change this element of your conduct and use silly terms rather than curse words, you will accomplish two valuable objectives. First, you will show your colleagues and clients that you respect them enough not to swear in front of them. Second, you also stand a pretty good chance of getting them to laugh and see your humorous side when you shout, "Blast!" Working to stop swearing and better express yourself in the professional setting will enhance your image among your coworkers and clients.

FACE-TO-FACE COMMUNICATION

Many of the rules of face-to-face communication are pretty obvious and may already be part of your personality. For example, you should avoid emotional topics of conversation (such as religion and politics) and use standard English (no slang, jargon, or vernacular).

When speaking to others, look them in the eye; this also goes for listening. When you look at a person with a desire to listen, you show that the individual is important to you and is worthy of your time. If you are tired or bored, fight the urge to yawn or glance away with an annoyed look on your face.

It is also a good idea to take along a pen and paper when you go to a meeting. You never know when someone will tell you something important that you need to remember. Even if your memory is great, write it down. Having a paper trail is helpful in business; it saves the embarrassment of having to ask a question twice. Another good alternative, if your phone has the capability, is to record a voice memo.

TELEPHONE ETIQUETTE

Because so much of business is conducted over the telephone, it is important to develop superior phone skills. Make sure to speak clearly and at a moderate pace. You do not want your clients to have to constantly ask you to repeat what you just said because you mumbled or spoke too quickly. Smile when you speak, be cordial, and even consider standing—it makes your voice sound stronger. Although it sounds crazy, people can hear the smile in your voice when you are on the telephone. Since many professionals today never meet their clients face to face, the telephone is their only link. For these people, a professional phone voice and demeanor are incredibly important. To be sure you are making the proper impression, ask your family, friends, and coworkers to listen to how you sound on the phone. If you think you need help, consider hiring a voice coach. A voice coach is not very expensive, and he or she can really help you improve your telephone and speaking skills.

During the course of a long business day, there are, understandably, many tasks that just don't get done. But returning phone calls — even those you do not want to make — is one of the things you must do every day. By being one of the few professionals who returns all phone calls, you will set yourself above the many people in business who think (incorrectly) that they are too busy to return calls.

PERSONAL CALLS

While at the office, you may need to make a few personal calls over the course of the day. Although most employers are willing to allow personal calls, be sure to keep them to a minimum, because they detract from your productivity. If your boss constantly hears you making personal calls, it will hurt your career. If subordinates hear you making personal calls, it will weaken your credibility and encourage them to do the same.

The speakerphone is a fantastic invention that has helped people accomplish other tasks while on the phone. Unfortunately, it is not appropriate for most business calls. If you receive permission from the person you're talking to, you may use the speakerphone; more often than not, its use is considered rude. The other party does not know if your coworkers are listening to the conversation, what else is going on, or why he or she is not important enough to get your complete attention. So, unless you are sitting on hold, use the receiver or a headset.

CELL PHONE ETIQUETTE

We've all seen rude people babbling on their cell phones in public places, from restaurants to public transportation, and even in movie theaters. The wireless headsets so many people wear have made this phenomenon even more prevalent and annoying. Cell phones infiltrated society faster than we could establish some basic rules for their use. What follows is a general guide that anyone can use to become more civilized and considerate when using mobile phones.

The first basic rule is that when you are in a public place or in the company of people you consider important, turn the ringer on your phone off. Your phone has voice mail, and you'll be well served by eliminating these interruptions. If you absolutely must take a call, set the phone on vibrate and politely excuse yourself to answer the call.

If you find yourself needing to talk in a public place, keep the conversation short and quiet. Remember how annoying it is to have to listen to a long, one-sided phone conversation, so keep it short. Ask the other person if you can talk at a better time and end the call.

If you find yourself driving and talking on the phone, realize that it is smarter, and safer, to pull over to finish the call. You might also consider purchasing a hands-free unit for your phone. Statistics show that talking on a cell phone while driving is just as dangerous as driving while intoxicated. Some cities have passed laws against driving while talking on a cell phone, so play it safe and pull over—or get a headset.

Fifteen years ago, cell phones were only for the business elite and for emergencies. Now that so many people are using them in so many different places, it is imperative that we all follow general rules of etiquette. Treat the people around you as though they are more important than anything else occurring at that moment, including your phone, and your etiquette will be evident.

WRITTEN COMMUNICATION

Many first impressions are made through written communication. The way you communicate through the written word gives others an idea of your intelligence, schooling, and business acumen. Although these assumptions may not be accurate, they quickly become a part of the impression you create. Becoming a great writer takes years of hard work, but there are some elements that everyone should follow. Whether you are a wordsmith painting a written picture or someone who writes only to convey information, using standard communication guidelines is essential to good etiquette.

The most famous and popular book on proper style is *The Elements of Style*, often referred to simply by the surnames of the authors, Strunk and White. This book contains a complete discussion of proper communication, from business to personal correspondence. It is a great reference tool and a must-have for the professional.

Regardless of what form of communication you choose (e-mail, letters, cards, etc.), be sure to proofread the item before you send it out. Although your computer's spell-checker will pick up some errors, it may not get words that are spelled correctly but used incorrectly—or a grammatical mistake. If the document is very important, you should have another person review it. Often, when you get close to a document, you will gloss over mistakes because you know what you want to say. Another person will help catch these mistakes.

It is also advisable to use a very readable font in your correspondence. Many computers now come with hundreds of fancy and ornate fonts. Although artistic, some of the more complicated choices are less desirable than a basic, readable font. Layout can vary with each form, but there are basic guidelines that should be followed, especially in your first few years in business.

THE BUSINESS LETTER

The business letter is less common in the modern era, but is still an important part of professional communication. By following the proper format, you will illustrate your knowledge of business culture and get your message across effectively. It is best to align all type on the left. Begin your letter with the date, followed by the name and address of the individual to whom you are writing. Next, greet the reader by the name you commonly use in conversation. If you have not met, do not use their first name. Make the letter as clear, straightforward, and easy to read as possible. In the first or second sentence, convey the purpose of writing, and spend the rest of the letter discussing the point.

Do your best to keep the letter to one page; 95 percent of all your communications should be limited to one page. Single-space the type but include an extra space between paragraphs. You may or may not indent the first line of each paragraph; that is a matter of personal style. When you complete the body of the text, conclude with "Sincerely," or "Best regards." Leave a few spaces for your signature and then type your full name.

In business correspondence, it is important to encourage the recipients to contact you with a "call to action." Even though your contact information is included in the letterhead, add a direct phone number or e-mail address for immediate contact and encourage the recipient to use it. This makes you appear more accessible and will make it easier for others to communicate with you.

THE BUSINESS MEMO

While used less frequently now, a business memorandum is still common in some offices. The proper
format for a memo is constantly changing, but the
following is a basic template.

First, type "MEMORANDUM" in capitals to
signify the format. Next, justify all type on the left,
and begin with the date. Then skip three lines and
identify the recipient by his or her complete name
preceded by "To:". Next, type "From:" and your full
name. Below the names, type "Re:" or "Subj:" and
indicate the reason for your communication. This
should be a three- or four- word phrase describing
the memo. Then write the body of the memo, leaving
spaces between paragraphs and not indenting their
first lines. No conclusion is necessary. Again, keep
your memo to one page. After you have printed it,
initial to the right of your name.

THANK-YOU NOTES

There will be times when you need to write a personal thank-you note to a colleague, client, or prospective client. When you receive a gift, secure a new
client, or have a great business dinner, it is a good
idea to thank the person. This can be done in a few

different ways, but the most effective is to make the note as personal as possible. Address your note by hand, including the return address, and use a stamp instead of a postage meter. Write the note on blank stationery or on a thank-you card instead of on your letterhead. Remember, this is your personal thank-you note. Write a few simple sentences that thank the person, describe the gift (or dinner), and encourage further contact. This simple tool can help build your career and keep you on top of your etiquette.

At Greenleaf Book Group, we send Thanksgiving cards and gifts to clients, vendors, and friends. It's not a religious holiday (and therefore will not offend any recipient) and it's before the standard giving season, so it stands out—plus, we really are thankful for our clients and vendors. Even the most powerful can benefit from sending thoughtful notes; President George H. W. Bush was famous for sending five handwritten cards per day to people he met.

E-MAIL COMMUNICATION

E-mail is now the most common form of communication in the workplace. Many employees use the Internet and communicate with friends and family all over the world on company time. Some employers condone this; others do not. Be sure to check your company's policy on personal e-mail during working hours before unnecessarily endangering your job.

With e-mail, you should always include a "signature," which will follow any message you send. It should include at a minimum your name and phone number but can also include your title, company, website, or other pertinent information. Remember to keep your signature relatively short—no one wants to read a long chunk of text at the end of your e-mail full of quotes, legal notices, and other text, so only include these if you are required to do so.

Begin your e-mail with the proper salutation, use professional language, and keep it short. Shorthand or "text-speak" isn't appropriate for business e-mails, but respect the time of the person to whom you are writing—keep to the point and be brief.

Problems can arise when employees believe that the e-mail messages they send at the office are private. By law, your employer can read all e-mail that you send and receive at work. It is unclear how many companies check messages, but the important point is that the possibility exists, and you must be aware of it. When using e-mail at work, assume that your boss and everyone else will read every word you write. If you aren't comfortable with that possibility, send your e-mails from home on your personal account.

If you feel the need to send personal e-mails, establish a personal account through an Internet service provider or a free portal like Google or Yahoo. Realize, though, that the same laws exist for surfing the Internet and visiting the web. Your employer can track the time you spend and the locations you visit on the Internet when using your company's system, so be careful. If you do visit sites that you would not want the entire office to know about, surf the web away from work. Failing to do so could definitely be a career-limiting move.

CONCLUSION

With the simple techniques discussed in this book, you can begin to take command of your professional demeanor. People will notice your attention to detail and realize that you care about your reputation. If you keep your appearance in order and act like a gentleman, you will undoubtedly find that you are treated with respect. But most important, you will feel more comfortable about yourself—and be able to do your best work. Remember, attention to detail can be a great help to your career and your life.

APPENDIX: GOLF ETIQUETTE

A great deal of business is conducted on the golf course, and knowing the proper etiquette can help you seal the deal. At the same time, you can quickly make a fool out of yourself if you stumble over the rules, both written and unwritten. Although a complete guide on golf etiquette could take volumes, this chapter should give you some of the basics.

First, you need to understand why golf and business are so closely tied. It is a simple fact that in about four hours on a golf course you can learn a great deal about those with whom you play. Integrity, skill under pressure, personal habits, risk-tolerance levels, and etiquette are all exposed. Golf is a surrogate for spending years getting to know someone. In this somewhat competitive arena, shrouded with class and dignity, a person's true nature is usually exposed. Think of it as a mini-battle; your true mettle is tested and you either win or lose.

Ambiguity in golf is not an option. Almost every professional should have a general understanding of the game of golf and its rules. It is also advisable to take a few lessons so that you'll have a basic level of competence if you are invited to play. Although it may not be your game of choice, it is often chosen in the business world. You will limit your chances for improvement, promotions, and new business by not knowing the basics.

GOLF TERMS

Golf terminology is unlike that used in other sports — it does not make a whole lot of sense. Scoring is based on the total number of *strokes* (times you hit the ball) you take in the *round* (eighteen holes of play); the lower the better. *Par* is the number of strokes it should take you to hit the ball from the *tee box* (where you start) to the *fairway* (the middle section), to the *green* (the area around the hole), and into the hole. There are three basic kinds of holes: par 3s, 4s, and 5s. The higher the par number, the longer the hole is in yards. If you *shoot* (score) par on a hole, you've done well. One over par is a *bogey*, two over is a *double bogey*, and so on. If you are one under par, you've made a *birdie*. If, somehow, you make two under par, you've got an *eagle* and have done a wonderful job. (You might want to consider retiring and trying out for the PGA tour if this becomes a regular occurrence.) You might also hear, or have to yell, "Fore!" This is a standard golf warning meaning that a ball is coming at you at a high rate of speed. The standard response is to hit the deck and cover your head. Although you might look a bit silly diving down, not heeding this warning can be quite painful.

DRESSING AND ACTING THE PART

Dressing for golf is a huge part of the game. The late Payne Stewart was one of the only modern professional golfers to wear old-style knickers. Although dressing in these early styles is not necessary, dressing properly for modern golf is mandatory. This means a collared shirt and slacks (not jeans), although in some hot-weather climates, shorts are acceptable. If you are unsure, call the club or your host to see if shorts can be worn. You should bring golf shoes with you, but wear your street shoes to the club and change in the locker room, not in the parking lot.

Keep just a few items in your pockets: two extra

balls, some tees, a divot repair tool (a divot is the piece of turf cut out of the ground by the club during a stroke), and a ball marker—a small, coin-like disc with a pin on the bottom, used to mark your ball's position if it needs to be cleaned or moved out of an opponent's way. You can use a dime as a marker, but be sure it does not make noise in your pocket. You should also keep some cash on you; gambling is not mandatory on the course, but it is often present and you must be prepared in case you lose.

Cell phones have become the scourge of the golf course as more and more golfers spend quite a lot of time talking on them during rounds. Although it is commendable that these golfers want to be reachable and get work done during their downtime, the golf course is not the place. If you have something important going on that is constantly interrupting the game, you should not be playing. Many private courses are cell phone–free zones, and some have even installed blocking devices that will jam any signals on the course. Although you will probably not be asked to leave if your phone rings, it is considered extremely poor etiquette to place or receive calls during the round. If you need the security of your phone, turn it off or make it silent and keep it in your bag. If you then find the need to use your phone, be sure to clear it with your host or those with whom you are playing before you start talking. Keep it short and only talk between holes, but if at all possible, save it for the clubhouse after the round. At worst, wait until you reach the halfway house where you can get a drink or snack. As the name implies, the halfway house, a rest stop where refreshments are often served, splits the *front* (first) nine holes and the *back* (last) nine holes.

RULES

When playing golf, there are a few rules to keep in mind. First and foremost, *do not cheat*. This may seem obvious, but it bears repeating. Remember, businesspeople use golf as a way of getting to know you, so any breach of honesty or integrity will reflect poorly on your character and your professional reputation. Count your score honestly; if you don't, others will. They might not yell out, "Liar! You had a seven— not a five!" but they will not forget that you shaved your score. This also applies to your *lie*, or the place the ball sits on the course. Often, players will nudge it onto a nice patch of grass, away from a stone or branch. Someone almost always sees this, and it is definitely against the rules.

There are two exceptions to this rule. One occurs when your ball lands in a "ground under repair" area, usually marked by a white circle. The other exception is if you are playing under the northern phenomenon of "winter rules," a variation on the normal regulations that is used in early spring and late fall. Although not officially recognized by the PGA, winter rules basically state that if the ball lies in a weather-damaged area like a huge puddle, you can move it out of the area, but no closer to the hole, without a penalty. If there's any question, you can always ask your partners for a ruling to make sure they believe you're playing fairly.

You will sometimes hear other players suggest that you "take a better lie" or "hit that one over." Do not accept these offers. Simply smile and say, "Thanks, but I think I can play that." Although it might add a few strokes to your game, it will earn you some great etiquette points.

Do not be afraid to ask questions when you are confused. If the rules or betting seem beyond your scope of understanding (and many bets are extremely complicated), ask for clarification. It is much harder to get clarification after you have broken a rule or lost a bet, and more damaging to the ego. This also applies to the course itself. If you are unsure of the layout of the hole, ask someone who has played there before. You might say something like, "If I'm somehow able to hit the ball properly, where should I aim?" Self-effacing humor, remember, is a great way to get others to help you.

Other rules of golf etiquette are common sense. For example, do not talk or make noise while someone is swinging or putting. You might ruin their concentration and lose a friend. If you make a divot during your swing, replace it and pat it down. Some courses will give you a green sand mixture that has grass seed in it to pour on top of the divot as well. When on the green, repair ball marks that you or others have left. It is very annoying to have a putt go offline because someone did not take care of the green.

When someone is hitting, there are two acceptable places to stand: directly behind the person so he or she cannot see you or at least seven feet in front of the person, facing his or her right shoulder. Never stand directly behind (or for that matter in front of) the line of flight of the ball. You will either distract the other person or get hit; neither option is very appealing.

If you have the misfortune of hitting your ball into a sand trap, remember to rake it clean after you hit the ball out. If one of your fellow golfers is stuck in a sand trap, it is considered good etiquette to hand him or her a rake after the shot to make the job easier for him. (A quick golf rule: If you are in the trap, also called a *hazard*, you may not let your club hit the sand until you swing at the ball. A real stickler for the rules might just catch you off guard, so be careful!)

Although there are hundreds of other rules that are considered good etiquette, these will help you get a start. The benefits that come from a well-played round of golf are more than worth the time it takes to learn the basics. If you can become a good "corporate golfer" who follows the rules and displays proper etiquette, you will reap the rewards tenfold.

SELECTED BIBLIOGRAPHY

Baldridge, Letitia. *Complete Guide to Executive Manners*. New York: Rawson Associates, 1985.

Bailey, Bill. *Golf Etiquette 101*. Roseville, CA: Prima, 1998.

Bridges, John. *How to Be a Gentleman*. Nashville, TN: Rutledge Hill Press, 1998.

Davis, Jeannie. *Beyond Hello*. Denver, CO: Now Hear This Publishing, 1999.

Dunnan, Nancy, and Nancy Tuckerman. *The Amy Vanderbilt Complete Book of Etiquette*. New York: Doubleday, 1995

Flusser, Alan. *Style and the Man*. New York: HarperStyle, 1996.

Friedman, Steve. *The Gentleman's Guide to Life*. New York: Three Rivers Press, 1997.

Grant, Lynella. *The Business Card Book*. Tucson, AZ: Off the Page Press, 1998.

Greenleaf, Clinton T. III. *Attention to Detail: A Gentleman's Guide to Professional Appearance and*

Conduct. Cleveland, OH: Greenleaf Enterprises, Inc., 1998.

———. *A Gentleman's Guide to Appearance.* Avon, MA: Adams Media, 2000.

———. *A Gentleman's Guide to Etiquette.* Avon, MA: Adams Media, 2001.

Greenleaf, Clinton T., III, and Stefani Schaefer. *Attention to Detail: A Woman's Guide to Professional Appearance and Conduct.* Cleveland, OH: Greenleaf Enterprises, Inc., 1999.

Gross, Kim Johnson, and Jeff Stone. *Men's Wardrobe (Chic Simple).* New York: Knopf, 1998.

Karlen, Josh, and Christopher Sulavik. *The Indispensable Guide to Classic Men's Clothing.* New York: Tatra Press, 1999.

Kohnen, Ryan. *Young Professional's Guide to Success.* San Antonio, TX: YP Success, 2009.

Meehan, Tim. *Suit Yourself.* Birmingham, AL: J.T. Meehan Publishing, 1999.

Omelanuk, Scott, and Ted Allen. *Esquire's Things a Man Should Know About Style.* New York: Riverhead Books, 1999.

Pincus, Marilyn. *Everyday Business Etiquette.* New York: Barron's, 1996.

Post, Peggy. *Emily Post's Etiquette*. New York: Harper-Collins, 1997.

Sabath, Ann Marie. *Business Etiquette: 101 Ways to Conduct Business with Charm and Savvy*. Franklin Lakes, NJ: Career Press, 1998.

Stewart, Marjabelle Young. *Executive Etiquette*. New York: St. Martin's Griffin, 1996.

ABOUT THE AUTHOR

Clint was in the Marine ROTC program at Holy Cross before graduating with an accounting degree and going to work at Deloitte as a staff accountant. He earned his CPA and retired from accounting at age twenty-two. Clint is the CEO of Greenleaf Book Group, which he founded in 1997 after writing and publishing two books, selling foreign publication rights, and securing a multi-book contract with Adams Media. Since then, he has built the company into one of the industry's leading book distributors. Greenleaf Book Group has represented more than one thousand titles, including four *New York Times* bestsellers and seven *Wall Street Journal* bestsellers, and appeared on *Inc.* magazine's list of the 500 fastest-growing companies in America. Clint sits on the AOL Small Business Board of Directors and the University of Texas Libraries Board, blogs for Inc. com, and is a regular guest host on Fox Business Network. He has been featured in the *Wall Street Journal, Inc.* magazine, Fox, MSBNC, *Money* magazine, *Men's Health*, *Forbes*, and *Entrepreneur*. Clint speaks about publishing and entrepreneurship across the country and internationally at conferences, seminars, and schools.